www.targettrg.co.uk
www.jcrmjournals.com

Published in 2020 by JCRM Journals, UK

Designed and Produced by Ralph & Claire Moody

ISBN: 979-8650360803

Grow Your Confidence With Public Speaking : Change your life with reflection and action.

Available from Amazon and other leading retail outlets.

If you would like us to create a bespoke journal for your organisation or work role contact us on +44 0800 302 9344.

If you enjoyed this journal please leave us a review on Amazon. Thank you.

www.jcrmjournals.com

Retail enquiries to:
info@targettrg.co.uk

Grow Your Confidence With Public Speaking

Change your life with reflection and action

RALPH & CLAIRE MOODY

www.targettrg.co.uk
www.jcrmjournals.com

In case of loss please return to:

....

....

....

www.targettrg.co.uk

www.jcrmjournals.com

GROW YOUR CONFIDENCE
WITH PUBLIC SPEAKING

CHANGE YOUR LIFE WITH REFLECTION
AND ACTION.

Our journals are designed to help individuals in any specific area they would like to change in their lives, both professionally and personally. We use coaching questions to guide your thinking in a different way.

Public speaking is the most common of all phobias. 75% of people suffer from speech anxiety, that is 3 out of 4 individuals suffer from anxiety when public speaking.

Self-Reflection to grow your confidence with public speaking

A journal is perfect to write your reflections every day. All you need to do is write for five minutes at the beginning or end of every day or both if you choose. Writing in a journal can create significant changes in your life when done correctly. We have both benefitted when writing a journal as do millions of others. It's an excellent opportunity to create a habit and build this into your life and as an example, make it part of your daily routine.

The purpose of this journal is to encourage you to reflect and develop when speaking in public, to create a focus for the best development. It's an opportunity to really understand yourself. Our journals are different they look at your thinking around the moments of decision making. It is getting to the route of the problem that creates the change looking past the specifics. We have written specific questions for you to use as a guide; these will help you in particular areas. If you sit with just thinking you will not notice as much as if you write. We felt a 50-session journal to begin with where you put all your reflections together would keep things simple for you. If you force yourself to write every day with your thoughts, you will grow in so many ways. You will be so much more successful in your life if you do this properly. Our aim with this journal is to encourage you to grow and focus to create change. A journal is perfect to record this; keeping all your thoughts and feelings in one place, incredibly powerful and very special.

Try not to make it a tick box exercise, so it becomes a chore. Make it something you look forward to doing, writing your thoughts and feelings on paper so you can reflect and look back. Create the habit and then watch how you develop and grow.

The journal includes a page for every day for you to make notes, then separate reflection sheets for every 5 sessions and then the final page. Reflection is so critical when writing your journal to see what words keep jumping out. If you find yourself writing the same things recognise this, then think why am I doing this, what change would I like?

Then you can reflect on this and what you can do differently. This will help you think in different ways and what you would like to be different, giving you a focus. Think about how you think and feel, you want to notice differences in yourself to create change, change will be happening if you pay attention.

Forcing yourself to write in a journal will create much more awareness about how you can develop yourself, your mindset and your patterns. There is no doubt you will find yourself developing in public speaking. It is little changes that move you to create bigger changes, you have to be committed though.

Writing a journal is an amazing journey, good luck and enjoy the very special thoughts and moments as you watch yourself develop when public speaking.

Ralph & Claire

Ralph & Claire Moody
Founders of JCRM Journals

HOW TO USE THE JOURNAL

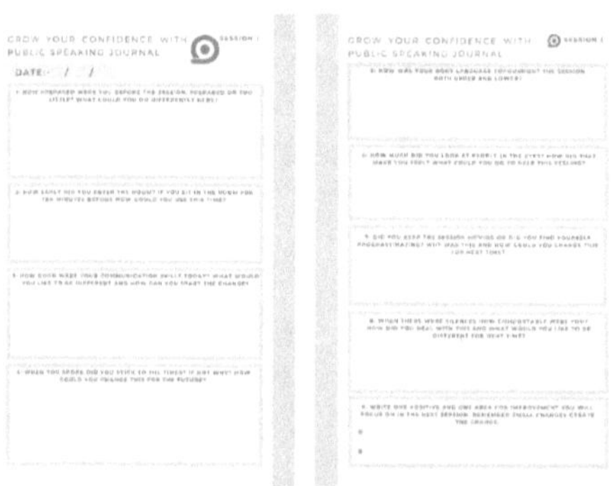

The session sheets are for you to complete after each session. Make sure you complete all questions.

Every 5 sessions complete a review of your actions and reflect on what you have achieved. We've included some public speaking tips too!

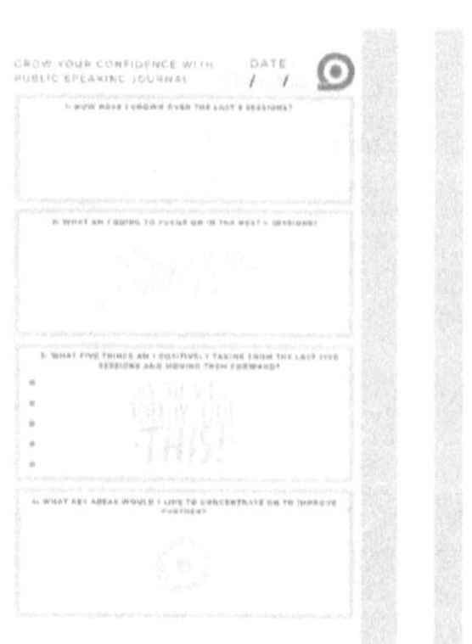

Before we start the journal some pre questions:

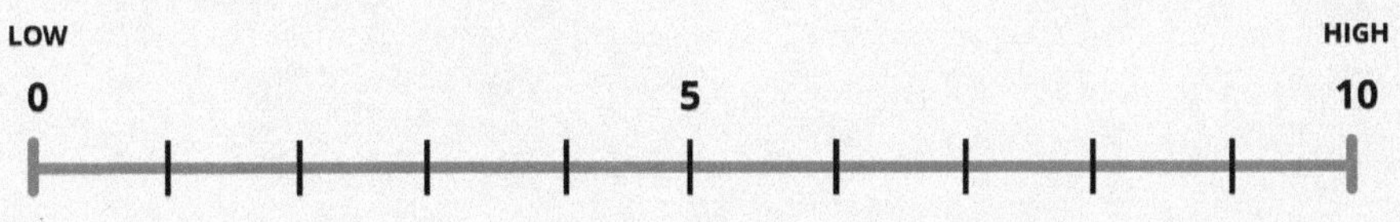

**BY THE END OF THE JOURNAL WHAT WOULD YOU LIKE TO BE DIFFERENT?
DRAW YOURSELF WHEN PUBLIC SPEAKING.**

GROW YOUR CONFIDENCE WITH PUBLIC SPEAKING JOURNAL

DATE:-   /   /

1: HOW PREPARED WERE YOU BEFORE THE SESSION, PREPARED OR TOO LITTLE? WHAT COULD YOU DO DIFFERENTLY HERE?

2: HOW EARLY DID YOU ENTER THE ROOM? IF YOU SIT IN THE ROOM FOR TEN MINUTES BEFORE HOW COULD YOU USE THIS TIME?

3: HOW GOOD WERE YOUR COMMUNICATION SKILLS TODAY? WHAT WOULD YOU LIKE TO BE DIFFERENT AND HOW CAN YOU START THE CHANGE?

4: WHEN YOU SPOKE DID YOU STICK TO THE TIMES? IF NOT WHY? HOW COULD YOU CHANGE THIS FOR THE FUTURE?

5: HOW WAS YOUR BODY LANGUAGE THROUGHOUT THE SESSION BOTH UPPER AND LOWER?

6: HOW MUCH DID YOU LOOK AT PEOPLE IN THE EYES? HOW DID THAT MAKE YOU FEEL? WHAT COULD YOU DO TO HELP THIS FEELING?

7: DID YOU KEEP THE SESSION MOVING OR DID YOU FIND YOURSELF PROCRASTINATING? WHY WAS THIS AND HOW COULD YOU CHANGE THIS FOR NEXT TIME?

8: WHEN THERE WERE SILENCES HOW COMFORTABLE WERE YOU? HOW DID YOU DEAL WITH THIS AND WHAT WOULD YOU LIKE TO BE DIFFERENT FOR NEXT TIME?

9: WRITE ONE POSITIVE AND ONE AREA FOR IMPROVEMENT YOU WILL FOCUS ON IN THE NEXT SESSION. REMEMBER SMALL CHANGES CREATE THE CHANGE.

-
-

GROW YOUR CONFIDENCE WITH PUBLIC SPEAKING JOURNAL

DATE:-   /   /

1: HOW PREPARED WERE YOU BEFORE THE SESSION, PREPARED OR TOO LITTLE? WHAT COULD YOU DO DIFFERENTLY HERE?

2: HOW EARLY DID YOU ENTER THE ROOM? IF YOU SIT IN THE ROOM FOR TEN MINUTES BEFORE HOW COULD YOU USE THIS TIME?

3: HOW GOOD WERE YOUR COMMUNICATION SKILLS TODAY? WHAT WOULD YOU LIKE TO BE DIFFERENT AND HOW CAN YOU START THE CHANGE?

4: WHEN YOU SPOKE DID YOU STICK TO THE TIMES? IF NOT WHY? HOW COULD YOU CHANGE THIS FOR THE FUTURE?

5: HOW WAS YOUR BODY LANGUAGE THROUGHOUT THE SESSION BOTH UPPER AND LOWER?

6: HOW MUCH DID YOU LOOK AT PEOPLE IN THE EYES? HOW DID THAT MAKE YOU FEEL? WHAT COULD YOU DO TO HELP THIS FEELING?

7: DID YOU KEEP THE SESSION MOVING OR DID YOU FIND YOURSELF PROCRASTINATING? WHY WAS THIS AND HOW COULD YOU CHANGE THIS FOR NEXT TIME?

8: WHEN THERE WERE SILENCES HOW COMFORTABLE WERE YOU? HOW DID YOU DEAL WITH THIS AND WHAT WOULD YOU LIKE TO BE DIFFERENT FOR NEXT TIME?

9: WRITE ONE POSITIVE AND ONE AREA FOR IMPROVEMENT YOU WILL FOCUS ON IN THE NEXT SESSION. REMEMBER SMALL CHANGES CREATE THE CHANGE.

-
-

GROW YOUR CONFIDENCE WITH PUBLIC SPEAKING JOURNAL

DATE:-   /   /

1: HOW PREPARED WERE YOU BEFORE THE SESSION, PREPARED OR TOO LITTLE? WHAT COULD YOU DO DIFFERENTLY HERE?

2: HOW EARLY DID YOU ENTER THE ROOM? IF YOU SIT IN THE ROOM FOR TEN MINUTES BEFORE HOW COULD YOU USE THIS TIME?

3: HOW GOOD WERE YOUR COMMUNICATION SKILLS TODAY? WHAT WOULD YOU LIKE TO BE DIFFERENT AND HOW CAN YOU START THE CHANGE?

4: WHEN YOU SPOKE DID YOU STICK TO THE TIMES? IF NOT WHY? HOW COULD YOU CHANGE THIS FOR THE FUTURE?

 **SESSION 3**

5: HOW WAS YOUR BODY LANGUAGE THROUGHOUT THE SESSION BOTH UPPER AND LOWER?

6: HOW MUCH DID YOU LOOK AT PEOPLE IN THE EYES? HOW DID THAT MAKE YOU FEEL? WHAT COULD YOU DO TO HELP THIS FEELING?

7: DID YOU KEEP THE SESSION MOVING OR DID YOU FIND YOURSELF PROCRASTINATING? WHY WAS THIS AND HOW COULD YOU CHANGE THIS FOR NEXT TIME?

8: WHEN THERE WERE SILENCES HOW COMFORTABLE WERE YOU? HOW DID YOU DEAL WITH THIS AND WHAT WOULD YOU LIKE TO BE DIFFERENT FOR NEXT TIME?

9: WRITE ONE POSITIVE AND ONE AREA FOR IMPROVEMENT YOU WILL FOCUS ON IN THE NEXT SESSION. REMEMBER SMALL CHANGES CREATE THE CHANGE.

-
-

GROW YOUR CONFIDENCE WITH PUBLIC SPEAKING JOURNAL

DATE:-   /   /

1: HOW PREPARED WERE YOU BEFORE THE SESSION, PREPARED OR TOO LITTLE? WHAT COULD YOU DO DIFFERENTLY HERE?

2: HOW EARLY DID YOU ENTER THE ROOM? IF YOU SIT IN THE ROOM FOR TEN MINUTES BEFORE HOW COULD YOU USE THIS TIME?

3: HOW GOOD WERE YOUR COMMUNICATION SKILLS TODAY? WHAT WOULD YOU LIKE TO BE DIFFERENT AND HOW CAN YOU START THE CHANGE?

4: WHEN YOU SPOKE DID YOU STICK TO THE TIMES? IF NOT WHY? HOW COULD YOU CHANGE THIS FOR THE FUTURE?

5: HOW WAS YOUR BODY LANGUAGE THROUGHOUT THE SESSION BOTH UPPER AND LOWER?

6: HOW MUCH DID YOU LOOK AT PEOPLE IN THE EYES? HOW DID THAT MAKE YOU FEEL? WHAT COULD YOU DO TO HELP THIS FEELING?

7: DID YOU KEEP THE SESSION MOVING OR DID YOU FIND YOURSELF PROCRASTINATING? WHY WAS THIS AND HOW COULD YOU CHANGE THIS FOR NEXT TIME?

8: WHEN THERE WERE SILENCES HOW COMFORTABLE WERE YOU? HOW DID YOU DEAL WITH THIS AND WHAT WOULD YOU LIKE TO BE DIFFERENT FOR NEXT TIME?

9: WRITE ONE POSITIVE AND ONE AREA FOR IMPROVEMENT YOU WILL FOCUS ON IN THE NEXT SESSION. REMEMBER SMALL CHANGES CREATE THE CHANGE.

-
-

GROW YOUR CONFIDENCE WITH PUBLIC SPEAKING JOURNAL

DATE:-   /   /

1: HOW PREPARED WERE YOU BEFORE THE SESSION, PREPARED OR TOO LITTLE? WHAT COULD YOU DO DIFFERENTLY HERE?

2: HOW EARLY DID YOU ENTER THE ROOM? IF YOU SIT IN THE ROOM FOR TEN MINUTES BEFORE HOW COULD YOU USE THIS TIME?

3: HOW GOOD WERE YOUR COMMUNICATION SKILLS TODAY? WHAT WOULD YOU LIKE TO BE DIFFERENT AND HOW CAN YOU START THE CHANGE?

4: WHEN YOU SPOKE DID YOU STICK TO THE TIMES? IF NOT WHY? HOW COULD YOU CHANGE THIS FOR THE FUTURE?

5: HOW WAS YOUR BODY LANGUAGE THROUGHOUT THE SESSION BOTH UPPER AND LOWER?

6: HOW MUCH DID YOU LOOK AT PEOPLE IN THE EYES? HOW DID THAT MAKE YOU FEEL? WHAT COULD YOU DO TO HELP THIS FEELING?

7: DID YOU KEEP THE SESSION MOVING OR DID YOU FIND YOURSELF PROCRASTINATING? WHY WAS THIS AND HOW COULD YOU CHANGE THIS FOR NEXT TIME?

8: WHEN THERE WERE SILENCES HOW COMFORTABLE WERE YOU? HOW DID YOU DEAL WITH THIS AND WHAT WOULD YOU LIKE TO BE DIFFERENT FOR NEXT TIME?

9: WRITE ONE POSITIVE AND ONE AREA FOR IMPROVEMENT YOU WILL FOCUS ON IN THE NEXT SESSION. REMEMBER SMALL CHANGES CREATE THE CHANGE.

-
-

GROW YOUR CONFIDENCE WITH PUBLIC SPEAKING JOURNAL

1: HOW HAVE I GROWN OVER THE LAST 5 SESSIONS?

2: WHAT AM I GOING TO FOCUS ON IN THE NEXT 5 SESSIONS?

3: WHAT FIVE THINGS AM I POSITIVELY TAKING FROM THE LAST FIVE SESSIONS AND MOVING THEM FORWARD?

-
-
-
-
-

4: WHAT KEY AREAS WOULD I LIKE TO CONCENTRATE ON TO IMPROVE FURTHER?

Reading PowerPoint Slides - Remember when we just read PowerPoint slides we are just telling. This isn't effective public speaking and likely that most of the delegates are fast asleep. PowerPoint is a visual aid to reinforce the key point we are trying to make .

GROW YOUR CONFIDENCE WITH PUBLIC SPEAKING JOURNAL

DATE:-   /   /

1: HOW PREPARED WERE YOU BEFORE THE SESSION, PREPARED OR TOO LITTLE? WHAT COULD YOU DO DIFFERENTLY HERE?

2: HOW EARLY DID YOU ENTER THE ROOM? IF YOU SIT IN THE ROOM FOR TEN MINUTES BEFORE HOW COULD YOU USE THIS TIME?

3: HOW GOOD WERE YOUR COMMUNICATION SKILLS TODAY? WHAT WOULD YOU LIKE TO BE DIFFERENT AND HOW CAN YOU START THE CHANGE?

4: WHEN YOU SPOKE DID YOU STICK TO THE TIMES? IF NOT WHY? HOW COULD YOU CHANGE THIS FOR THE FUTURE?

5: HOW WAS YOUR BODY LANGUAGE THROUGHOUT THE SESSION BOTH UPPER AND LOWER?

6: HOW MUCH DID YOU LOOK AT PEOPLE IN THE EYES? HOW DID THAT MAKE YOU FEEL? WHAT COULD YOU DO TO HELP THIS FEELING?

7: DID YOU KEEP THE SESSION MOVING OR DID YOU FIND YOURSELF PROCRASTINATING? WHY WAS THIS AND HOW COULD YOU CHANGE THIS FOR NEXT TIME?

8: WHEN THERE WERE SILENCES HOW COMFORTABLE WERE YOU? HOW DID YOU DEAL WITH THIS AND WHAT WOULD YOU LIKE TO BE DIFFERENT FOR NEXT TIME?

9: WRITE ONE POSITIVE AND ONE AREA FOR IMPROVEMENT YOU WILL FOCUS ON IN THE NEXT SESSION. REMEMBER SMALL CHANGES CREATE THE CHANGE.

-
-

GROW YOUR CONFIDENCE WITH PUBLIC SPEAKING JOURNAL

DATE:-   /   /

1: HOW PREPARED WERE YOU BEFORE THE SESSION, PREPARED OR TOO LITTLE? WHAT COULD YOU DO DIFFERENTLY HERE?

2: HOW EARLY DID YOU ENTER THE ROOM? IF YOU SIT IN THE ROOM FOR TEN MINUTES BEFORE HOW COULD YOU USE THIS TIME?

3: HOW GOOD WERE YOUR COMMUNICATION SKILLS TODAY? WHAT WOULD YOU LIKE TO BE DIFFERENT AND HOW CAN YOU START THE CHANGE?

4: WHEN YOU SPOKE DID YOU STICK TO THE TIMES? IF NOT WHY? HOW COULD YOU CHANGE THIS FOR THE FUTURE?

5: HOW WAS YOUR BODY LANGUAGE THROUGHOUT THE SESSION BOTH UPPER AND LOWER?

6: HOW MUCH DID YOU LOOK AT PEOPLE IN THE EYES? HOW DID THAT MAKE YOU FEEL? WHAT COULD YOU DO TO HELP THIS FEELING?

7: DID YOU KEEP THE SESSION MOVING OR DID YOU FIND YOURSELF PROCRASTINATING? WHY WAS THIS AND HOW COULD YOU CHANGE THIS FOR NEXT TIME?

8: WHEN THERE WERE SILENCES HOW COMFORTABLE WERE YOU? HOW DID YOU DEAL WITH THIS AND WHAT WOULD YOU LIKE TO BE DIFFERENT FOR NEXT TIME?

9: WRITE ONE POSITIVE AND ONE AREA FOR IMPROVEMENT YOU WILL FOCUS ON IN THE NEXT SESSION. REMEMBER SMALL CHANGES CREATE THE CHANGE.

-
-

GROW YOUR CONFIDENCE WITH PUBLIC SPEAKING JOURNAL

DATE:- / /

1: HOW PREPARED WERE YOU BEFORE THE SESSION, PREPARED OR TOO LITTLE? WHAT COULD YOU DO DIFFERENTLY HERE?

2: HOW EARLY DID YOU ENTER THE ROOM? IF YOU SIT IN THE ROOM FOR TEN MINUTES BEFORE HOW COULD YOU USE THIS TIME?

3: HOW GOOD WERE YOUR COMMUNICATION SKILLS TODAY? WHAT WOULD YOU LIKE TO BE DIFFERENT AND HOW CAN YOU START THE CHANGE?

4: WHEN YOU SPOKE DID YOU STICK TO THE TIMES? IF NOT WHY? HOW COULD YOU CHANGE THIS FOR THE FUTURE?

5: HOW WAS YOUR BODY LANGUAGE THROUGHOUT THE SESSION BOTH UPPER AND LOWER?

6: HOW MUCH DID YOU LOOK AT PEOPLE IN THE EYES? HOW DID THAT MAKE YOU FEEL? WHAT COULD YOU DO TO HELP THIS FEELING?

7: DID YOU KEEP THE SESSION MOVING OR DID YOU FIND YOURSELF PROCRASTINATING? WHY WAS THIS AND HOW COULD YOU CHANGE THIS FOR NEXT TIME?

8: WHEN THERE WERE SILENCES HOW COMFORTABLE WERE YOU? HOW DID YOU DEAL WITH THIS AND WHAT WOULD YOU LIKE TO BE DIFFERENT FOR NEXT TIME?

9: WRITE ONE POSITIVE AND ONE AREA FOR IMPROVEMENT YOU WILL FOCUS ON IN THE NEXT SESSION. REMEMBER SMALL CHANGES CREATE THE CHANGE.

GROW YOUR CONFIDENCE WITH PUBLIC SPEAKING JOURNAL

DATE:-   /   /

1: HOW PREPARED WERE YOU BEFORE THE SESSION, PREPARED OR TOO LITTLE? WHAT COULD YOU DO DIFFERENTLY HERE?

2: HOW EARLY DID YOU ENTER THE ROOM? IF YOU SIT IN THE ROOM FOR TEN MINUTES BEFORE HOW COULD YOU USE THIS TIME?

3: HOW GOOD WERE YOUR COMMUNICATION SKILLS TODAY? WHAT WOULD YOU LIKE TO BE DIFFERENT AND HOW CAN YOU START THE CHANGE?

4: WHEN YOU SPOKE DID YOU STICK TO THE TIMES? IF NOT WHY? HOW COULD YOU CHANGE THIS FOR THE FUTURE?

5: HOW WAS YOUR BODY LANGUAGE THROUGHOUT THE SESSION BOTH UPPER AND LOWER?

6: HOW MUCH DID YOU LOOK AT PEOPLE IN THE EYES? HOW DID THAT MAKE YOU FEEL? WHAT COULD YOU DO TO HELP THIS FEELING?

7: DID YOU KEEP THE SESSION MOVING OR DID YOU FIND YOURSELF PROCRASTINATING? WHY WAS THIS AND HOW COULD YOU CHANGE THIS FOR NEXT TIME?

8: WHEN THERE WERE SILENCES HOW COMFORTABLE WERE YOU? HOW DID YOU DEAL WITH THIS AND WHAT WOULD YOU LIKE TO BE DIFFERENT FOR NEXT TIME?

9: WRITE ONE POSITIVE AND ONE AREA FOR IMPROVEMENT YOU WILL FOCUS ON IN THE NEXT SESSION. REMEMBER SMALL CHANGES CREATE THE CHANGE.

GROW YOUR CONFIDENCE WITH PUBLIC SPEAKING JOURNAL

DATE:-   /   /

1: HOW PREPARED WERE YOU BEFORE THE SESSION, PREPARED OR TOO LITTLE? WHAT COULD YOU DO DIFFERENTLY HERE?

2: HOW EARLY DID YOU ENTER THE ROOM? IF YOU SIT IN THE ROOM FOR TEN MINUTES BEFORE HOW COULD YOU USE THIS TIME?

3: HOW GOOD WERE YOUR COMMUNICATION SKILLS TODAY? WHAT WOULD YOU LIKE TO BE DIFFERENT AND HOW CAN YOU START THE CHANGE?

4: WHEN YOU SPOKE DID YOU STICK TO THE TIMES? IF NOT WHY? HOW COULD YOU CHANGE THIS FOR THE FUTURE?

5: HOW WAS YOUR BODY LANGUAGE THROUGHOUT THE SESSION BOTH UPPER AND LOWER?

6: HOW MUCH DID YOU LOOK AT PEOPLE IN THE EYES? HOW DID THAT MAKE YOU FEEL? WHAT COULD YOU DO TO HELP THIS FEELING?

7: DID YOU KEEP THE SESSION MOVING OR DID YOU FIND YOURSELF PROCRASTINATING? WHY WAS THIS AND HOW COULD YOU CHANGE THIS FOR NEXT TIME?

8: WHEN THERE WERE SILENCES HOW COMFORTABLE WERE YOU? HOW DID YOU DEAL WITH THIS AND WHAT WOULD YOU LIKE TO BE DIFFERENT FOR NEXT TIME?

9: WRITE ONE POSITIVE AND ONE AREA FOR IMPROVEMENT YOU WILL FOCUS ON IN THE NEXT SESSION. REMEMBER SMALL CHANGES CREATE THE CHANGE.

-
-

1: HOW HAVE I GROWN OVER THE LAST 5 SESSIONS?

2: WHAT AM I GOING TO FOCUS ON IN THE NEXT 5 SESSIONS?

3: WHAT FIVE THINGS AM I POSITIVELY TAKING FROM THE LAST FIVE SESSIONS AND MOVING THEM FORWARD?

-
-
-
-
-

4: WHAT KEY AREAS WOULD I LIKE TO CONCENTRATE ON TO IMPROVE FURTHER?

Structure - A good presentation has a Beginning, a Middle and an End or an Intro, a Main Body and a Summary. Without structure chaos always wins.

GROW YOUR CONFIDENCE WITH PUBLIC SPEAKING JOURNAL

DATE:-   /   /

1: HOW PREPARED WERE YOU BEFORE THE SESSION, PREPARED OR TOO LITTLE? WHAT COULD YOU DO DIFFERENTLY HERE?

2: HOW EARLY DID YOU ENTER THE ROOM? IF YOU SIT IN THE ROOM FOR TEN MINUTES BEFORE HOW COULD YOU USE THIS TIME?

3: HOW GOOD WERE YOUR COMMUNICATION SKILLS TODAY? WHAT WOULD YOU LIKE TO BE DIFFERENT AND HOW CAN YOU START THE CHANGE?

4: WHEN YOU SPOKE DID YOU STICK TO THE TIMES? IF NOT WHY? HOW COULD YOU CHANGE THIS FOR THE FUTURE?

5: HOW WAS YOUR BODY LANGUAGE THROUGHOUT THE SESSION BOTH UPPER AND LOWER?

6: HOW MUCH DID YOU LOOK AT PEOPLE IN THE EYES? HOW DID THAT MAKE YOU FEEL? WHAT COULD YOU DO TO HELP THIS FEELING?

7: DID YOU KEEP THE SESSION MOVING OR DID YOU FIND YOURSELF PROCRASTINATING? WHY WAS THIS AND HOW COULD YOU CHANGE THIS FOR NEXT TIME?

8: WHEN THERE WERE SILENCES HOW COMFORTABLE WERE YOU? HOW DID YOU DEAL WITH THIS AND WHAT WOULD YOU LIKE TO BE DIFFERENT FOR NEXT TIME?

9: WRITE ONE POSITIVE AND ONE AREA FOR IMPROVEMENT YOU WILL FOCUS ON IN THE NEXT SESSION. REMEMBER SMALL CHANGES CREATE THE CHANGE.

GROW YOUR CONFIDENCE WITH PUBLIC SPEAKING JOURNAL

DATE:-   /   /

1: HOW PREPARED WERE YOU BEFORE THE SESSION, PREPARED OR TOO LITTLE? WHAT COULD YOU DO DIFFERENTLY HERE?

2: HOW EARLY DID YOU ENTER THE ROOM? IF YOU SIT IN THE ROOM FOR TEN MINUTES BEFORE HOW COULD YOU USE THIS TIME?

3: HOW GOOD WERE YOUR COMMUNICATION SKILLS TODAY? WHAT WOULD YOU LIKE TO BE DIFFERENT AND HOW CAN YOU START THE CHANGE?

4: WHEN YOU SPOKE DID YOU STICK TO THE TIMES? IF NOT WHY? HOW COULD YOU CHANGE THIS FOR THE FUTURE?

5: HOW WAS YOUR BODY LANGUAGE THROUGHOUT THE SESSION BOTH UPPER AND LOWER?

6: HOW MUCH DID YOU LOOK AT PEOPLE IN THE EYES? HOW DID THAT MAKE YOU FEEL? WHAT COULD YOU DO TO HELP THIS FEELING?

7: DID YOU KEEP THE SESSION MOVING OR DID YOU FIND YOURSELF PROCRASTINATING? WHY WAS THIS AND HOW COULD YOU CHANGE THIS FOR NEXT TIME?

8: WHEN THERE WERE SILENCES HOW COMFORTABLE WERE YOU? HOW DID YOU DEAL WITH THIS AND WHAT WOULD YOU LIKE TO BE DIFFERENT FOR NEXT TIME?

9: WRITE ONE POSITIVE AND ONE AREA FOR IMPROVEMENT YOU WILL FOCUS ON IN THE NEXT SESSION. REMEMBER SMALL CHANGES CREATE THE CHANGE.

-
-

DATE:-   /   /

1: HOW PREPARED WERE YOU BEFORE THE SESSION, PREPARED OR TOO LITTLE? WHAT COULD YOU DO DIFFERENTLY HERE?

2: HOW EARLY DID YOU ENTER THE ROOM? IF YOU SIT IN THE ROOM FOR TEN MINUTES BEFORE HOW COULD YOU USE THIS TIME?

3: HOW GOOD WERE YOUR COMMUNICATION SKILLS TODAY? WHAT WOULD YOU LIKE TO BE DIFFERENT AND HOW CAN YOU START THE CHANGE?

4: WHEN YOU SPOKE DID YOU STICK TO THE TIMES? IF NOT WHY? HOW COULD YOU CHANGE THIS FOR THE FUTURE?

5: HOW WAS YOUR BODY LANGUAGE THROUGHOUT THE SESSION BOTH UPPER AND LOWER?

6: HOW MUCH DID YOU LOOK AT PEOPLE IN THE EYES? HOW DID THAT MAKE YOU FEEL? WHAT COULD YOU DO TO HELP THIS FEELING?

7: DID YOU KEEP THE SESSION MOVING OR DID YOU FIND YOURSELF PROCRASTINATING? WHY WAS THIS AND HOW COULD YOU CHANGE THIS FOR NEXT TIME?

8: WHEN THERE WERE SILENCES HOW COMFORTABLE WERE YOU? HOW DID YOU DEAL WITH THIS AND WHAT WOULD YOU LIKE TO BE DIFFERENT FOR NEXT TIME?

9: WRITE ONE POSITIVE AND ONE AREA FOR IMPROVEMENT YOU WILL FOCUS ON IN THE NEXT SESSION. REMEMBER SMALL CHANGES CREATE THE CHANGE.

DATE:-   /   /

1: HOW PREPARED WERE YOU BEFORE THE SESSION, PREPARED OR TOO LITTLE? WHAT COULD YOU DO DIFFERENTLY HERE?

2: HOW EARLY DID YOU ENTER THE ROOM? IF YOU SIT IN THE ROOM FOR TEN MINUTES BEFORE HOW COULD YOU USE THIS TIME?

3: HOW GOOD WERE YOUR COMMUNICATION SKILLS TODAY? WHAT WOULD YOU LIKE TO BE DIFFERENT AND HOW CAN YOU START THE CHANGE?

4: WHEN YOU SPOKE DID YOU STICK TO THE TIMES? IF NOT WHY? HOW COULD YOU CHANGE THIS FOR THE FUTURE?

GROW YOUR CONFIDENCE WITH PUBLIC SPEAKING JOURNAL

5: HOW WAS YOUR BODY LANGUAGE THROUGHOUT THE SESSION BOTH UPPER AND LOWER?

6: HOW MUCH DID YOU LOOK AT PEOPLE IN THE EYES? HOW DID THAT MAKE YOU FEEL? WHAT COULD YOU DO TO HELP THIS FEELING?

7: DID YOU KEEP THE SESSION MOVING OR DID YOU FIND YOURSELF PROCRASTINATING? WHY WAS THIS AND HOW COULD YOU CHANGE THIS FOR NEXT TIME?

8: WHEN THERE WERE SILENCES HOW COMFORTABLE WERE YOU? HOW DID YOU DEAL WITH THIS AND WHAT WOULD YOU LIKE TO BE DIFFERENT FOR NEXT TIME?

9: WRITE ONE POSITIVE AND ONE AREA FOR IMPROVEMENT YOU WILL FOCUS ON IN THE NEXT SESSION. REMEMBER SMALL CHANGES CREATE THE CHANGE.

GROW YOUR CONFIDENCE WITH PUBLIC SPEAKING JOURNAL

DATE:-   /   /

1: HOW PREPARED WERE YOU BEFORE THE SESSION, PREPARED OR TOO LITTLE? WHAT COULD YOU DO DIFFERENTLY HERE?

2: HOW EARLY DID YOU ENTER THE ROOM? IF YOU SIT IN THE ROOM FOR TEN MINUTES BEFORE HOW COULD YOU USE THIS TIME?

3: HOW GOOD WERE YOUR COMMUNICATION SKILLS TODAY? WHAT WOULD YOU LIKE TO BE DIFFERENT AND HOW CAN YOU START THE CHANGE?

4: WHEN YOU SPOKE DID YOU STICK TO THE TIMES? IF NOT WHY? HOW COULD YOU CHANGE THIS FOR THE FUTURE?

5: HOW WAS YOUR BODY LANGUAGE THROUGHOUT THE SESSION BOTH UPPER AND LOWER?

6: HOW MUCH DID YOU LOOK AT PEOPLE IN THE EYES? HOW DID THAT MAKE YOU FEEL? WHAT COULD YOU DO TO HELP THIS FEELING?

7: DID YOU KEEP THE SESSION MOVING OR DID YOU FIND YOURSELF PROCRASTINATING? WHY WAS THIS AND HOW COULD YOU CHANGE THIS FOR NEXT TIME?

8: WHEN THERE WERE SILENCES HOW COMFORTABLE WERE YOU? HOW DID YOU DEAL WITH THIS AND WHAT WOULD YOU LIKE TO BE DIFFERENT FOR NEXT TIME?

9: WRITE ONE POSITIVE AND ONE AREA FOR IMPROVEMENT YOU WILL FOCUS ON IN THE NEXT SESSION. REMEMBER SMALL CHANGES CREATE THE CHANGE.

-
-

DATE:- / /

1: HOW HAVE I GROWN OVER THE LAST 5 SESSIONS?

2: WHAT AM I GOING TO FOCUS ON IN THE NEXT 5 SESSIONS?

3: WHAT FIVE THINGS AM I POSITIVELY TAKING FROM THE LAST FIVE SESSIONS AND MOVING THEM FORWARD?

-
-
-
-
-

4: WHAT KEY AREAS WOULD I LIKE TO CONCENTRATE ON TO IMPROVE FURTHER?

Body Language - Really good open body language looks confident and also looks natural. Body language should be open throughout including the bottom half of your body, no crossing legs, arms or having your back to the audience.

GROW YOUR CONFIDENCE WITH PUBLIC SPEAKING JOURNAL

DATE:-   /   /

1: HOW PREPARED WERE YOU BEFORE THE SESSION, PREPARED OR TOO LITTLE? WHAT COULD YOU DO DIFFERENTLY HERE?

2: HOW EARLY DID YOU ENTER THE ROOM? IF YOU SIT IN THE ROOM FOR TEN MINUTES BEFORE HOW COULD YOU USE THIS TIME?

3: HOW GOOD WERE YOUR COMMUNICATION SKILLS TODAY? WHAT WOULD YOU LIKE TO BE DIFFERENT AND HOW CAN YOU START THE CHANGE?

4: WHEN YOU SPOKE DID YOU STICK TO THE TIMES? IF NOT WHY? HOW COULD YOU CHANGE THIS FOR THE FUTURE?

5: HOW WAS YOUR BODY LANGUAGE THROUGHOUT THE SESSION BOTH UPPER AND LOWER?

6: HOW MUCH DID YOU LOOK AT PEOPLE IN THE EYES? HOW DID THAT MAKE YOU FEEL? WHAT COULD YOU DO TO HELP THIS FEELING?

7: DID YOU KEEP THE SESSION MOVING OR DID YOU FIND YOURSELF PROCRASTINATING? WHY WAS THIS AND HOW COULD YOU CHANGE THIS FOR NEXT TIME?

8: WHEN THERE WERE SILENCES HOW COMFORTABLE WERE YOU? HOW DID YOU DEAL WITH THIS AND WHAT WOULD YOU LIKE TO BE DIFFERENT FOR NEXT TIME?

9: WRITE ONE POSITIVE AND ONE AREA FOR IMPROVEMENT YOU WILL FOCUS ON IN THE NEXT SESSION. REMEMBER SMALL CHANGES CREATE THE CHANGE.

-
-

GROW YOUR CONFIDENCE WITH PUBLIC SPEAKING JOURNAL

DATE:-   /   /

1: HOW PREPARED WERE YOU BEFORE THE SESSION, PREPARED OR TOO LITTLE? WHAT COULD YOU DO DIFFERENTLY HERE?

2: HOW EARLY DID YOU ENTER THE ROOM? IF YOU SIT IN THE ROOM FOR TEN MINUTES BEFORE HOW COULD YOU USE THIS TIME?

3: HOW GOOD WERE YOUR COMMUNICATION SKILLS TODAY? WHAT WOULD YOU LIKE TO BE DIFFERENT AND HOW CAN YOU START THE CHANGE?

4: WHEN YOU SPOKE DID YOU STICK TO THE TIMES? IF NOT WHY? HOW COULD YOU CHANGE THIS FOR THE FUTURE?

5: HOW WAS YOUR BODY LANGUAGE THROUGHOUT THE SESSION BOTH UPPER AND LOWER?

6: HOW MUCH DID YOU LOOK AT PEOPLE IN THE EYES? HOW DID THAT MAKE YOU FEEL? WHAT COULD YOU DO TO HELP THIS FEELING?

7: DID YOU KEEP THE SESSION MOVING OR DID YOU FIND YOURSELF PROCRASTINATING? WHY WAS THIS AND HOW COULD YOU CHANGE THIS FOR NEXT TIME?

8: WHEN THERE WERE SILENCES HOW COMFORTABLE WERE YOU? HOW DID YOU DEAL WITH THIS AND WHAT WOULD YOU LIKE TO BE DIFFERENT FOR NEXT TIME?

9: WRITE ONE POSITIVE AND ONE AREA FOR IMPROVEMENT YOU WILL FOCUS ON IN THE NEXT SESSION. REMEMBER SMALL CHANGES CREATE THE CHANGE.

GROW YOUR CONFIDENCE WITH PUBLIC SPEAKING JOURNAL

DATE:-   /   /

1: HOW PREPARED WERE YOU BEFORE THE SESSION, PREPARED OR TOO LITTLE? WHAT COULD YOU DO DIFFERENTLY HERE?

2: HOW EARLY DID YOU ENTER THE ROOM? IF YOU SIT IN THE ROOM FOR TEN MINUTES BEFORE HOW COULD YOU USE THIS TIME?

3: HOW GOOD WERE YOUR COMMUNICATION SKILLS TODAY? WHAT WOULD YOU LIKE TO BE DIFFERENT AND HOW CAN YOU START THE CHANGE?

4: WHEN YOU SPOKE DID YOU STICK TO THE TIMES? IF NOT WHY? HOW COULD YOU CHANGE THIS FOR THE FUTURE?

5: HOW WAS YOUR BODY LANGUAGE THROUGHOUT THE SESSION BOTH UPPER AND LOWER?

6: HOW MUCH DID YOU LOOK AT PEOPLE IN THE EYES? HOW DID THAT MAKE YOU FEEL? WHAT COULD YOU DO TO HELP THIS FEELING?

7: DID YOU KEEP THE SESSION MOVING OR DID YOU FIND YOURSELF PROCRASTINATING? WHY WAS THIS AND HOW COULD YOU CHANGE THIS FOR NEXT TIME?

8: WHEN THERE WERE SILENCES HOW COMFORTABLE WERE YOU? HOW DID YOU DEAL WITH THIS AND WHAT WOULD YOU LIKE TO BE DIFFERENT FOR NEXT TIME?

9: WRITE ONE POSITIVE AND ONE AREA FOR IMPROVEMENT YOU WILL FOCUS ON IN THE NEXT SESSION. REMEMBER SMALL CHANGES CREATE THE CHANGE.

GROW YOUR CONFIDENCE WITH PUBLIC SPEAKING JOURNAL

DATE:-   /   /

1: HOW PREPARED WERE YOU BEFORE THE SESSION, PREPARED OR TOO LITTLE? WHAT COULD YOU DO DIFFERENTLY HERE?

2: HOW EARLY DID YOU ENTER THE ROOM? IF YOU SIT IN THE ROOM FOR TEN MINUTES BEFORE HOW COULD YOU USE THIS TIME?

3: HOW GOOD WERE YOUR COMMUNICATION SKILLS TODAY? WHAT WOULD YOU LIKE TO BE DIFFERENT AND HOW CAN YOU START THE CHANGE?

4: WHEN YOU SPOKE DID YOU STICK TO THE TIMES? IF NOT WHY? HOW COULD YOU CHANGE THIS FOR THE FUTURE?

5: HOW WAS YOUR BODY LANGUAGE THROUGHOUT THE SESSION BOTH UPPER AND LOWER?

6: HOW MUCH DID YOU LOOK AT PEOPLE IN THE EYES? HOW DID THAT MAKE YOU FEEL? WHAT COULD YOU DO TO HELP THIS FEELING?

7: DID YOU KEEP THE SESSION MOVING OR DID YOU FIND YOURSELF PROCRASTINATING? WHY WAS THIS AND HOW COULD YOU CHANGE THIS FOR NEXT TIME?

8: WHEN THERE WERE SILENCES HOW COMFORTABLE WERE YOU? HOW DID YOU DEAL WITH THIS AND WHAT WOULD YOU LIKE TO BE DIFFERENT FOR NEXT TIME?

9: WRITE ONE POSITIVE AND ONE AREA FOR IMPROVEMENT YOU WILL FOCUS ON IN THE NEXT SESSION. REMEMBER SMALL CHANGES CREATE THE CHANGE.

-
-

GROW YOUR CONFIDENCE WITH PUBLIC SPEAKING JOURNAL

DATE:-   /   /

1: HOW PREPARED WERE YOU BEFORE THE SESSION, PREPARED OR TOO LITTLE? WHAT COULD YOU DO DIFFERENTLY HERE?

2: HOW EARLY DID YOU ENTER THE ROOM? IF YOU SIT IN THE ROOM FOR TEN MINUTES BEFORE HOW COULD YOU USE THIS TIME?

3: HOW GOOD WERE YOUR COMMUNICATION SKILLS TODAY? WHAT WOULD YOU LIKE TO BE DIFFERENT AND HOW CAN YOU START THE CHANGE?

4: WHEN YOU SPOKE DID YOU STICK TO THE TIMES? IF NOT WHY? HOW COULD YOU CHANGE THIS FOR THE FUTURE?

 SESSION 20

5: HOW WAS YOUR BODY LANGUAGE THROUGHOUT THE SESSION BOTH UPPER AND LOWER?

6: HOW MUCH DID YOU LOOK AT PEOPLE IN THE EYES? HOW DID THAT MAKE YOU FEEL? WHAT COULD YOU DO TO HELP THIS FEELING?

7: DID YOU KEEP THE SESSION MOVING OR DID YOU FIND YOURSELF PROCRASTINATING? WHY WAS THIS AND HOW COULD YOU CHANGE THIS FOR NEXT TIME?

8: WHEN THERE WERE SILENCES HOW COMFORTABLE WERE YOU? HOW DID YOU DEAL WITH THIS AND WHAT WOULD YOU LIKE TO BE DIFFERENT FOR NEXT TIME?

9: WRITE ONE POSITIVE AND ONE AREA FOR IMPROVEMENT YOU WILL FOCUS ON IN THE NEXT SESSION. REMEMBER SMALL CHANGES CREATE THE CHANGE.

DATE:- / /

1: HOW HAVE I GROWN OVER THE LAST 5 SESSIONS?

2: WHAT AM I GOING TO FOCUS ON IN THE NEXT 5 SESSIONS?

3: WHAT FIVE THINGS AM I POSITIVELY TAKING FROM THE LAST FIVE SESSIONS AND MOVING THEM FORWARD?

-
-
-
-
-

4: WHAT KEY AREAS WOULD I LIKE TO CONCENTRATE ON TO IMPROVE FURTHER?

Appear Natural - The best public speakers appear natural, even though they may not feel natural at all. Inside world war may be going on, but outside, we must make sure we appear to be natural and in control

GROW YOUR CONFIDENCE WITH PUBLIC SPEAKING JOURNAL

DATE:-   /   /

1: HOW PREPARED WERE YOU BEFORE THE SESSION, PREPARED OR TOO LITTLE? WHAT COULD YOU DO DIFFERENTLY HERE?

2: HOW EARLY DID YOU ENTER THE ROOM? IF YOU SIT IN THE ROOM FOR TEN MINUTES BEFORE HOW COULD YOU USE THIS TIME?

3: HOW GOOD WERE YOUR COMMUNICATION SKILLS TODAY? WHAT WOULD YOU LIKE TO BE DIFFERENT AND HOW CAN YOU START THE CHANGE?

4: WHEN YOU SPOKE DID YOU STICK TO THE TIMES? IF NOT WHY? HOW COULD YOU CHANGE THIS FOR THE FUTURE?

5: HOW WAS YOUR BODY LANGUAGE THROUGHOUT THE SESSION BOTH UPPER AND LOWER?

6: HOW MUCH DID YOU LOOK AT PEOPLE IN THE EYES? HOW DID THAT MAKE YOU FEEL? WHAT COULD YOU DO TO HELP THIS FEELING?

7: DID YOU KEEP THE SESSION MOVING OR DID YOU FIND YOURSELF PROCRASTINATING? WHY WAS THIS AND HOW COULD YOU CHANGE THIS FOR NEXT TIME?

8: WHEN THERE WERE SILENCES HOW COMFORTABLE WERE YOU? HOW DID YOU DEAL WITH THIS AND WHAT WOULD YOU LIKE TO BE DIFFERENT FOR NEXT TIME?

9: WRITE ONE POSITIVE AND ONE AREA FOR IMPROVEMENT YOU WILL FOCUS ON IN THE NEXT SESSION. REMEMBER SMALL CHANGES CREATE THE CHANGE.

-
-

GROW YOUR CONFIDENCE WITH PUBLIC SPEAKING JOURNAL

DATE:-   /   /

1: HOW PREPARED WERE YOU BEFORE THE SESSION, PREPARED OR TOO LITTLE? WHAT COULD YOU DO DIFFERENTLY HERE?

2: HOW EARLY DID YOU ENTER THE ROOM? IF YOU SIT IN THE ROOM FOR TEN MINUTES BEFORE HOW COULD YOU USE THIS TIME?

3: HOW GOOD WERE YOUR COMMUNICATION SKILLS TODAY? WHAT WOULD YOU LIKE TO BE DIFFERENT AND HOW CAN YOU START THE CHANGE?

4: WHEN YOU SPOKE DID YOU STICK TO THE TIMES? IF NOT WHY? HOW COULD YOU CHANGE THIS FOR THE FUTURE?

5: HOW WAS YOUR BODY LANGUAGE THROUGHOUT THE SESSION BOTH UPPER AND LOWER?

6: HOW MUCH DID YOU LOOK AT PEOPLE IN THE EYES? HOW DID THAT MAKE YOU FEEL? WHAT COULD YOU DO TO HELP THIS FEELING?

7: DID YOU KEEP THE SESSION MOVING OR DID YOU FIND YOURSELF PROCRASTINATING? WHY WAS THIS AND HOW COULD YOU CHANGE THIS FOR NEXT TIME?

8: WHEN THERE WERE SILENCES HOW COMFORTABLE WERE YOU? HOW DID YOU DEAL WITH THIS AND WHAT WOULD YOU LIKE TO BE DIFFERENT FOR NEXT TIME?

9: WRITE ONE POSITIVE AND ONE AREA FOR IMPROVEMENT YOU WILL FOCUS ON IN THE NEXT SESSION. REMEMBER SMALL CHANGES CREATE THE CHANGE.

DATE:-   /   /

1: HOW PREPARED WERE YOU BEFORE THE SESSION, PREPARED OR TOO LITTLE? WHAT COULD YOU DO DIFFERENTLY HERE?

2: HOW EARLY DID YOU ENTER THE ROOM? IF YOU SIT IN THE ROOM FOR TEN MINUTES BEFORE HOW COULD YOU USE THIS TIME?

3: HOW GOOD WERE YOUR COMMUNICATION SKILLS TODAY? WHAT WOULD YOU LIKE TO BE DIFFERENT AND HOW CAN YOU START THE CHANGE?

4: WHEN YOU SPOKE DID YOU STICK TO THE TIMES? IF NOT WHY? HOW COULD YOU CHANGE THIS FOR THE FUTURE?

5: HOW WAS YOUR BODY LANGUAGE THROUGHOUT THE SESSION BOTH UPPER AND LOWER?

6: HOW MUCH DID YOU LOOK AT PEOPLE IN THE EYES? HOW DID THAT MAKE YOU FEEL? WHAT COULD YOU DO TO HELP THIS FEELING?

7: DID YOU KEEP THE SESSION MOVING OR DID YOU FIND YOURSELF PROCRASTINATING? WHY WAS THIS AND HOW COULD YOU CHANGE THIS FOR NEXT TIME?

8: WHEN THERE WERE SILENCES HOW COMFORTABLE WERE YOU? HOW DID YOU DEAL WITH THIS AND WHAT WOULD YOU LIKE TO BE DIFFERENT FOR NEXT TIME?

9: WRITE ONE POSITIVE AND ONE AREA FOR IMPROVEMENT YOU WILL FOCUS ON IN THE NEXT SESSION. REMEMBER SMALL CHANGES CREATE THE CHANGE.

-
-

GROW YOUR CONFIDENCE WITH PUBLIC SPEAKING JOURNAL

DATE:-   /   /

1: HOW PREPARED WERE YOU BEFORE THE SESSION, PREPARED OR TOO LITTLE? WHAT COULD YOU DO DIFFERENTLY HERE?

2: HOW EARLY DID YOU ENTER THE ROOM? IF YOU SIT IN THE ROOM FOR TEN MINUTES BEFORE HOW COULD YOU USE THIS TIME?

3: HOW GOOD WERE YOUR COMMUNICATION SKILLS TODAY? WHAT WOULD YOU LIKE TO BE DIFFERENT AND HOW CAN YOU START THE CHANGE?

4: WHEN YOU SPOKE DID YOU STICK TO THE TIMES? IF NOT WHY? HOW COULD YOU CHANGE THIS FOR THE FUTURE?

5: HOW WAS YOUR BODY LANGUAGE THROUGHOUT THE SESSION BOTH UPPER AND LOWER?

6: HOW MUCH DID YOU LOOK AT PEOPLE IN THE EYES? HOW DID THAT MAKE YOU FEEL? WHAT COULD YOU DO TO HELP THIS FEELING?

7: DID YOU KEEP THE SESSION MOVING OR DID YOU FIND YOURSELF PROCRASTINATING? WHY WAS THIS AND HOW COULD YOU CHANGE THIS FOR NEXT TIME?

8: WHEN THERE WERE SILENCES HOW COMFORTABLE WERE YOU? HOW DID YOU DEAL WITH THIS AND WHAT WOULD YOU LIKE TO BE DIFFERENT FOR NEXT TIME?

9: WRITE ONE POSITIVE AND ONE AREA FOR IMPROVEMENT YOU WILL FOCUS ON IN THE NEXT SESSION. REMEMBER SMALL CHANGES CREATE THE CHANGE.

-
-

GROW YOUR CONFIDENCE WITH PUBLIC SPEAKING JOURNAL

DATE:-   /   /

1: HOW PREPARED WERE YOU BEFORE THE SESSION, PREPARED OR TOO LITTLE? WHAT COULD YOU DO DIFFERENTLY HERE?

2: HOW EARLY DID YOU ENTER THE ROOM? IF YOU SIT IN THE ROOM FOR TEN MINUTES BEFORE HOW COULD YOU USE THIS TIME?

3: HOW GOOD WERE YOUR COMMUNICATION SKILLS TODAY? WHAT WOULD YOU LIKE TO BE DIFFERENT AND HOW CAN YOU START THE CHANGE?

4: WHEN YOU SPOKE DID YOU STICK TO THE TIMES? IF NOT WHY? HOW COULD YOU CHANGE THIS FOR THE FUTURE?

5: HOW WAS YOUR BODY LANGUAGE THROUGHOUT THE SESSION BOTH UPPER AND LOWER?

6: HOW MUCH DID YOU LOOK AT PEOPLE IN THE EYES? HOW DID THAT MAKE YOU FEEL? WHAT COULD YOU DO TO HELP THIS FEELING?

7: DID YOU KEEP THE SESSION MOVING OR DID YOU FIND YOURSELF PROCRASTINATING? WHY WAS THIS AND HOW COULD YOU CHANGE THIS FOR NEXT TIME?

8: WHEN THERE WERE SILENCES HOW COMFORTABLE WERE YOU? HOW DID YOU DEAL WITH THIS AND WHAT WOULD YOU LIKE TO BE DIFFERENT FOR NEXT TIME?

9: WRITE ONE POSITIVE AND ONE AREA FOR IMPROVEMENT YOU WILL FOCUS ON IN THE NEXT SESSION. REMEMBER SMALL CHANGES CREATE THE CHANGE.

GROW YOUR CONFIDENCE WITH PUBLIC SPEAKING JOURNAL

1: HOW HAVE I GROWN OVER THE LAST 5 SESSIONS?

2: WHAT AM I GOING TO FOCUS ON IN THE NEXT 5 SESSIONS?

3: WHAT FIVE THINGS AM I POSITIVELY TAKING FROM THE LAST FIVE SESSIONS AND MOVING THEM FORWARD?

-
-
-
-
-

4: WHAT KEY AREAS WOULD I LIKE TO CONCENTRATE ON TO IMPROVE FURTHER?

Session 25

Congratulations

Congratulations for meeting the halfway point, tremendous effort and fantastic that you are growing in public speaking reflection. The book is for you only, very personnel and as you reflect on the last twenty five sessions, look at your incredible journey. Every little change is the change you need to move forward. Think about achieving your goal of increased reflection, what will it feel like at session 50, just imagine that feeling.

GROW YOUR CONFIDENCE WITH PUBLIC SPEAKING JOURNAL

DATE:-   /   /

1: HOW PREPARED WERE YOU BEFORE THE SESSION, PREPARED OR TOO LITTLE? WHAT COULD YOU DO DIFFERENTLY HERE?

2: HOW EARLY DID YOU ENTER THE ROOM? IF YOU SIT IN THE ROOM FOR TEN MINUTES BEFORE HOW COULD YOU USE THIS TIME?

3: HOW GOOD WERE YOUR COMMUNICATION SKILLS TODAY? WHAT WOULD YOU LIKE TO BE DIFFERENT AND HOW CAN YOU START THE CHANGE?

4: WHEN YOU SPOKE DID YOU STICK TO THE TIMES? IF NOT WHY? HOW COULD YOU CHANGE THIS FOR THE FUTURE?

5: HOW WAS YOUR BODY LANGUAGE THROUGHOUT THE SESSION BOTH UPPER AND LOWER?

6: HOW MUCH DID YOU LOOK AT PEOPLE IN THE EYES? HOW DID THAT MAKE YOU FEEL? WHAT COULD YOU DO TO HELP THIS FEELING?

7: DID YOU KEEP THE SESSION MOVING OR DID YOU FIND YOURSELF PROCRASTINATING? WHY WAS THIS AND HOW COULD YOU CHANGE THIS FOR NEXT TIME?

8: WHEN THERE WERE SILENCES HOW COMFORTABLE WERE YOU? HOW DID YOU DEAL WITH THIS AND WHAT WOULD YOU LIKE TO BE DIFFERENT FOR NEXT TIME?

9: WRITE ONE POSITIVE AND ONE AREA FOR IMPROVEMENT YOU WILL FOCUS ON IN THE NEXT SESSION. REMEMBER SMALL CHANGES CREATE THE CHANGE.

-
-

GROW YOUR CONFIDENCE WITH PUBLIC SPEAKING JOURNAL

DATE:-   /   /

1: HOW PREPARED WERE YOU BEFORE THE SESSION, PREPARED OR TOO LITTLE? WHAT COULD YOU DO DIFFERENTLY HERE?

2: HOW EARLY DID YOU ENTER THE ROOM? IF YOU SIT IN THE ROOM FOR TEN MINUTES BEFORE HOW COULD YOU USE THIS TIME?

3: HOW GOOD WERE YOUR COMMUNICATION SKILLS TODAY? WHAT WOULD YOU LIKE TO BE DIFFERENT AND HOW CAN YOU START THE CHANGE?

4: WHEN YOU SPOKE DID YOU STICK TO THE TIMES? IF NOT WHY? HOW COULD YOU CHANGE THIS FOR THE FUTURE?

5: HOW WAS YOUR BODY LANGUAGE THROUGHOUT THE SESSION BOTH UPPER AND LOWER?

6: HOW MUCH DID YOU LOOK AT PEOPLE IN THE EYES? HOW DID THAT MAKE YOU FEEL? WHAT COULD YOU DO TO HELP THIS FEELING?

7: DID YOU KEEP THE SESSION MOVING OR DID YOU FIND YOURSELF PROCRASTINATING? WHY WAS THIS AND HOW COULD YOU CHANGE THIS FOR NEXT TIME?

8: WHEN THERE WERE SILENCES HOW COMFORTABLE WERE YOU? HOW DID YOU DEAL WITH THIS AND WHAT WOULD YOU LIKE TO BE DIFFERENT FOR NEXT TIME?

9: WRITE ONE POSITIVE AND ONE AREA FOR IMPROVEMENT YOU WILL FOCUS ON IN THE NEXT SESSION. REMEMBER SMALL CHANGES CREATE THE CHANGE.

GROW YOUR CONFIDENCE WITH PUBLIC SPEAKING JOURNAL

DATE:-   /   /

1: HOW PREPARED WERE YOU BEFORE THE SESSION, PREPARED OR TOO LITTLE? WHAT COULD YOU DO DIFFERENTLY HERE?

2: HOW EARLY DID YOU ENTER THE ROOM? IF YOU SIT IN THE ROOM FOR TEN MINUTES BEFORE HOW COULD YOU USE THIS TIME?

3: HOW GOOD WERE YOUR COMMUNICATION SKILLS TODAY? WHAT WOULD YOU LIKE TO BE DIFFERENT AND HOW CAN YOU START THE CHANGE?

4: WHEN YOU SPOKE DID YOU STICK TO THE TIMES? IF NOT WHY? HOW COULD YOU CHANGE THIS FOR THE FUTURE?

 SESSION 28

5: HOW WAS YOUR BODY LANGUAGE THROUGHOUT THE SESSION BOTH UPPER AND LOWER?

6: HOW MUCH DID YOU LOOK AT PEOPLE IN THE EYES? HOW DID THAT MAKE YOU FEEL? WHAT COULD YOU DO TO HELP THIS FEELING?

7: DID YOU KEEP THE SESSION MOVING OR DID YOU FIND YOURSELF PROCRASTINATING? WHY WAS THIS AND HOW COULD YOU CHANGE THIS FOR NEXT TIME?

8: WHEN THERE WERE SILENCES HOW COMFORTABLE WERE YOU? HOW DID YOU DEAL WITH THIS AND WHAT WOULD YOU LIKE TO BE DIFFERENT FOR NEXT TIME?

9: WRITE ONE POSITIVE AND ONE AREA FOR IMPROVEMENT YOU WILL FOCUS ON IN THE NEXT SESSION. REMEMBER SMALL CHANGES CREATE THE CHANGE.

-
-

GROW YOUR CONFIDENCE WITH PUBLIC SPEAKING JOURNAL

DATE:-   /   /

1: HOW PREPARED WERE YOU BEFORE THE SESSION, PREPARED OR TOO LITTLE? WHAT COULD YOU DO DIFFERENTLY HERE?

2: HOW EARLY DID YOU ENTER THE ROOM? IF YOU SIT IN THE ROOM FOR TEN MINUTES BEFORE HOW COULD YOU USE THIS TIME?

3: HOW GOOD WERE YOUR COMMUNICATION SKILLS TODAY? WHAT WOULD YOU LIKE TO BE DIFFERENT AND HOW CAN YOU START THE CHANGE?

4: WHEN YOU SPOKE DID YOU STICK TO THE TIMES? IF NOT WHY? HOW COULD YOU CHANGE THIS FOR THE FUTURE?

5: HOW WAS YOUR BODY LANGUAGE THROUGHOUT THE SESSION BOTH UPPER AND LOWER?

6: HOW MUCH DID YOU LOOK AT PEOPLE IN THE EYES? HOW DID THAT MAKE YOU FEEL? WHAT COULD YOU DO TO HELP THIS FEELING?

7: DID YOU KEEP THE SESSION MOVING OR DID YOU FIND YOURSELF PROCRASTINATING? WHY WAS THIS AND HOW COULD YOU CHANGE THIS FOR NEXT TIME?

8: WHEN THERE WERE SILENCES HOW COMFORTABLE WERE YOU? HOW DID YOU DEAL WITH THIS AND WHAT WOULD YOU LIKE TO BE DIFFERENT FOR NEXT TIME?

9: WRITE ONE POSITIVE AND ONE AREA FOR IMPROVEMENT YOU WILL FOCUS ON IN THE NEXT SESSION. REMEMBER SMALL CHANGES CREATE THE CHANGE.

-
-

GROW YOUR CONFIDENCE WITH PUBLIC SPEAKING JOURNAL

DATE:-   /   /

1: HOW PREPARED WERE YOU BEFORE THE SESSION, PREPARED OR TOO LITTLE? WHAT COULD YOU DO DIFFERENTLY HERE?

2: HOW EARLY DID YOU ENTER THE ROOM? IF YOU SIT IN THE ROOM FOR TEN MINUTES BEFORE HOW COULD YOU USE THIS TIME?

3: HOW GOOD WERE YOUR COMMUNICATION SKILLS TODAY? WHAT WOULD YOU LIKE TO BE DIFFERENT AND HOW CAN YOU START THE CHANGE?

4: WHEN YOU SPOKE DID YOU STICK TO THE TIMES? IF NOT WHY? HOW COULD YOU CHANGE THIS FOR THE FUTURE?

5: HOW WAS YOUR BODY LANGUAGE THROUGHOUT THE SESSION BOTH UPPER AND LOWER?

6: HOW MUCH DID YOU LOOK AT PEOPLE IN THE EYES? HOW DID THAT MAKE YOU FEEL? WHAT COULD YOU DO TO HELP THIS FEELING?

7: DID YOU KEEP THE SESSION MOVING OR DID YOU FIND YOURSELF PROCRASTINATING? WHY WAS THIS AND HOW COULD YOU CHANGE THIS FOR NEXT TIME?

8: WHEN THERE WERE SILENCES HOW COMFORTABLE WERE YOU? HOW DID YOU DEAL WITH THIS AND WHAT WOULD YOU LIKE TO BE DIFFERENT FOR NEXT TIME?

9: WRITE ONE POSITIVE AND ONE AREA FOR IMPROVEMENT YOU WILL FOCUS ON IN THE NEXT SESSION. REMEMBER SMALL CHANGES CREATE THE CHANGE.

-
-

DATE:-  / /

1: HOW HAVE I GROWN OVER THE LAST 5 SESSIONS?

2: WHAT AM I GOING TO FOCUS ON IN THE NEXT 5 SESSIONS?

3: WHAT FIVE THINGS AM I POSITIVELY TAKING FROM THE LAST FIVE SESSIONS AND MOVING THEM FORWARD?

-
-
-
-
-

4: WHAT KEY AREAS WOULD I LIKE TO CONCENTRATE ON TO IMPROVE FURTHER?

Passion - Always deliver any presentation with passion. Audiences love passionate speakers as they find them more engaging. Be passionate and people will not switch off.

DATE:-   /   /

1: HOW PREPARED WERE YOU BEFORE THE SESSION, PREPARED OR TOO LITTLE? WHAT COULD YOU DO DIFFERENTLY HERE?

2: HOW EARLY DID YOU ENTER THE ROOM? IF YOU SIT IN THE ROOM FOR TEN MINUTES BEFORE HOW COULD YOU USE THIS TIME?

3: HOW GOOD WERE YOUR COMMUNICATION SKILLS TODAY? WHAT WOULD YOU LIKE TO BE DIFFERENT AND HOW CAN YOU START THE CHANGE?

4: WHEN YOU SPOKE DID YOU STICK TO THE TIMES? IF NOT WHY? HOW COULD YOU CHANGE THIS FOR THE FUTURE?

5: HOW WAS YOUR BODY LANGUAGE THROUGHOUT THE SESSION BOTH UPPER AND LOWER?

6: HOW MUCH DID YOU LOOK AT PEOPLE IN THE EYES? HOW DID THAT MAKE YOU FEEL? WHAT COULD YOU DO TO HELP THIS FEELING?

7: DID YOU KEEP THE SESSION MOVING OR DID YOU FIND YOURSELF PROCRASTINATING? WHY WAS THIS AND HOW COULD YOU CHANGE THIS FOR NEXT TIME?

8: WHEN THERE WERE SILENCES HOW COMFORTABLE WERE YOU? HOW DID YOU DEAL WITH THIS AND WHAT WOULD YOU LIKE TO BE DIFFERENT FOR NEXT TIME?

9: WRITE ONE POSITIVE AND ONE AREA FOR IMPROVEMENT YOU WILL FOCUS ON IN THE NEXT SESSION. REMEMBER SMALL CHANGES CREATE THE CHANGE.

-
-

GROW YOUR CONFIDENCE WITH PUBLIC SPEAKING JOURNAL

DATE:-   /   /

1: HOW PREPARED WERE YOU BEFORE THE SESSION, PREPARED OR TOO LITTLE? WHAT COULD YOU DO DIFFERENTLY HERE?

2: HOW EARLY DID YOU ENTER THE ROOM? IF YOU SIT IN THE ROOM FOR TEN MINUTES BEFORE HOW COULD YOU USE THIS TIME?

3: HOW GOOD WERE YOUR COMMUNICATION SKILLS TODAY? WHAT WOULD YOU LIKE TO BE DIFFERENT AND HOW CAN YOU START THE CHANGE?

4: WHEN YOU SPOKE DID YOU STICK TO THE TIMES? IF NOT WHY? HOW COULD YOU CHANGE THIS FOR THE FUTURE?

5: HOW WAS YOUR BODY LANGUAGE THROUGHOUT THE SESSION BOTH UPPER AND LOWER?

6: HOW MUCH DID YOU LOOK AT PEOPLE IN THE EYES? HOW DID THAT MAKE YOU FEEL? WHAT COULD YOU DO TO HELP THIS FEELING?

7: DID YOU KEEP THE SESSION MOVING OR DID YOU FIND YOURSELF PROCRASTINATING? WHY WAS THIS AND HOW COULD YOU CHANGE THIS FOR NEXT TIME?

8: WHEN THERE WERE SILENCES HOW COMFORTABLE WERE YOU? HOW DID YOU DEAL WITH THIS AND WHAT WOULD YOU LIKE TO BE DIFFERENT FOR NEXT TIME?

9: WRITE ONE POSITIVE AND ONE AREA FOR IMPROVEMENT YOU WILL FOCUS ON IN THE NEXT SESSION. REMEMBER SMALL CHANGES CREATE THE CHANGE.

-
-

DATE:-   /   /

1: HOW PREPARED WERE YOU BEFORE THE SESSION, PREPARED OR TOO LITTLE? WHAT COULD YOU DO DIFFERENTLY HERE?

2: HOW EARLY DID YOU ENTER THE ROOM? IF YOU SIT IN THE ROOM FOR TEN MINUTES BEFORE HOW COULD YOU USE THIS TIME?

3: HOW GOOD WERE YOUR COMMUNICATION SKILLS TODAY? WHAT WOULD YOU LIKE TO BE DIFFERENT AND HOW CAN YOU START THE CHANGE?

4: WHEN YOU SPOKE DID YOU STICK TO THE TIMES? IF NOT WHY? HOW COULD YOU CHANGE THIS FOR THE FUTURE?

5: HOW WAS YOUR BODY LANGUAGE THROUGHOUT THE SESSION BOTH UPPER AND LOWER?

6: HOW MUCH DID YOU LOOK AT PEOPLE IN THE EYES? HOW DID THAT MAKE YOU FEEL? WHAT COULD YOU DO TO HELP THIS FEELING?

7: DID YOU KEEP THE SESSION MOVING OR DID YOU FIND YOURSELF PROCRASTINATING? WHY WAS THIS AND HOW COULD YOU CHANGE THIS FOR NEXT TIME?

8: WHEN THERE WERE SILENCES HOW COMFORTABLE WERE YOU? HOW DID YOU DEAL WITH THIS AND WHAT WOULD YOU LIKE TO BE DIFFERENT FOR NEXT TIME?

9: WRITE ONE POSITIVE AND ONE AREA FOR IMPROVEMENT YOU WILL FOCUS ON IN THE NEXT SESSION. REMEMBER SMALL CHANGES CREATE THE CHANGE.

-
-

GROW YOUR CONFIDENCE WITH PUBLIC SPEAKING JOURNAL

DATE:-   /   /

1: HOW PREPARED WERE YOU BEFORE THE SESSION, PREPARED OR TOO LITTLE? WHAT COULD YOU DO DIFFERENTLY HERE?

2: HOW EARLY DID YOU ENTER THE ROOM? IF YOU SIT IN THE ROOM FOR TEN MINUTES BEFORE HOW COULD YOU USE THIS TIME?

3: HOW GOOD WERE YOUR COMMUNICATION SKILLS TODAY? WHAT WOULD YOU LIKE TO BE DIFFERENT AND HOW CAN YOU START THE CHANGE?

4: WHEN YOU SPOKE DID YOU STICK TO THE TIMES? IF NOT WHY? HOW COULD YOU CHANGE THIS FOR THE FUTURE?

 SESSION 34

5: HOW WAS YOUR BODY LANGUAGE THROUGHOUT THE SESSION BOTH UPPER AND LOWER?

6: HOW MUCH DID YOU LOOK AT PEOPLE IN THE EYES? HOW DID THAT MAKE YOU FEEL? WHAT COULD YOU DO TO HELP THIS FEELING?

7: DID YOU KEEP THE SESSION MOVING OR DID YOU FIND YOURSELF PROCRASTINATING? WHY WAS THIS AND HOW COULD YOU CHANGE THIS FOR NEXT TIME?

8: WHEN THERE WERE SILENCES HOW COMFORTABLE WERE YOU? HOW DID YOU DEAL WITH THIS AND WHAT WOULD YOU LIKE TO BE DIFFERENT FOR NEXT TIME?

9: WRITE ONE POSITIVE AND ONE AREA FOR IMPROVEMENT YOU WILL FOCUS ON IN THE NEXT SESSION. REMEMBER SMALL CHANGES CREATE THE CHANGE.

GROW YOUR CONFIDENCE WITH PUBLIC SPEAKING JOURNAL

DATE:-   /   /

1: HOW PREPARED WERE YOU BEFORE THE SESSION, PREPARED OR TOO LITTLE? WHAT COULD YOU DO DIFFERENTLY HERE?

2: HOW EARLY DID YOU ENTER THE ROOM? IF YOU SIT IN THE ROOM FOR TEN MINUTES BEFORE HOW COULD YOU USE THIS TIME?

3: HOW GOOD WERE YOUR COMMUNICATION SKILLS TODAY? WHAT WOULD YOU LIKE TO BE DIFFERENT AND HOW CAN YOU START THE CHANGE?

4: WHEN YOU SPOKE DID YOU STICK TO THE TIMES? IF NOT WHY? HOW COULD YOU CHANGE THIS FOR THE FUTURE?

5: HOW WAS YOUR BODY LANGUAGE THROUGHOUT THE SESSION BOTH UPPER AND LOWER?

6: HOW MUCH DID YOU LOOK AT PEOPLE IN THE EYES? HOW DID THAT MAKE YOU FEEL? WHAT COULD YOU DO TO HELP THIS FEELING?

7: DID YOU KEEP THE SESSION MOVING OR DID YOU FIND YOURSELF PROCRASTINATING? WHY WAS THIS AND HOW COULD YOU CHANGE THIS FOR NEXT TIME?

8: WHEN THERE WERE SILENCES HOW COMFORTABLE WERE YOU? HOW DID YOU DEAL WITH THIS AND WHAT WOULD YOU LIKE TO BE DIFFERENT FOR NEXT TIME?

9: WRITE ONE POSITIVE AND ONE AREA FOR IMPROVEMENT YOU WILL FOCUS ON IN THE NEXT SESSION. REMEMBER SMALL CHANGES CREATE THE CHANGE.

-
-

1: HOW HAVE I GROWN OVER THE LAST 5 SESSIONS?

2: WHAT AM I GOING TO FOCUS ON IN THE NEXT 5 SESSIONS?

3: WHAT FIVE THINGS AM I POSITIVELY TAKING FROM THE LAST FIVE SESSIONS AND MOVING THEM FORWARD?

-
-
-
-
-

4: WHAT KEY AREAS WOULD I LIKE TO CONCENTRATE ON TO IMPROVE FURTHER?

Be Prepared - Never assume that everything will work and that organisers will have all the right cables etc. Be prepared and check before. If you fail to prepare then you prepare to fail.

GROW YOUR CONFIDENCE WITH PUBLIC SPEAKING JOURNAL

DATE:-   /   /

1: HOW PREPARED WERE YOU BEFORE THE SESSION, PREPARED OR TOO LITTLE? WHAT COULD YOU DO DIFFERENTLY HERE?

2: HOW EARLY DID YOU ENTER THE ROOM? IF YOU SIT IN THE ROOM FOR TEN MINUTES BEFORE HOW COULD YOU USE THIS TIME?

3: HOW GOOD WERE YOUR COMMUNICATION SKILLS TODAY? WHAT WOULD YOU LIKE TO BE DIFFERENT AND HOW CAN YOU START THE CHANGE?

4: WHEN YOU SPOKE DID YOU STICK TO THE TIMES? IF NOT WHY? HOW COULD YOU CHANGE THIS FOR THE FUTURE?

5: HOW WAS YOUR BODY LANGUAGE THROUGHOUT THE SESSION BOTH UPPER AND LOWER?

6: HOW MUCH DID YOU LOOK AT PEOPLE IN THE EYES? HOW DID THAT MAKE YOU FEEL? WHAT COULD YOU DO TO HELP THIS FEELING?

7: DID YOU KEEP THE SESSION MOVING OR DID YOU FIND YOURSELF PROCRASTINATING? WHY WAS THIS AND HOW COULD YOU CHANGE THIS FOR NEXT TIME?

8: WHEN THERE WERE SILENCES HOW COMFORTABLE WERE YOU? HOW DID YOU DEAL WITH THIS AND WHAT WOULD YOU LIKE TO BE DIFFERENT FOR NEXT TIME?

9: WRITE ONE POSITIVE AND ONE AREA FOR IMPROVEMENT YOU WILL FOCUS ON IN THE NEXT SESSION. REMEMBER SMALL CHANGES CREATE THE CHANGE.

-
-

GROW YOUR CONFIDENCE WITH PUBLIC SPEAKING JOURNAL

DATE:-   /   /

1: HOW PREPARED WERE YOU BEFORE THE SESSION, PREPARED OR TOO LITTLE? WHAT COULD YOU DO DIFFERENTLY HERE?

2: HOW EARLY DID YOU ENTER THE ROOM? IF YOU SIT IN THE ROOM FOR TEN MINUTES BEFORE HOW COULD YOU USE THIS TIME?

3: HOW GOOD WERE YOUR COMMUNICATION SKILLS TODAY? WHAT WOULD YOU LIKE TO BE DIFFERENT AND HOW CAN YOU START THE CHANGE?

4: WHEN YOU SPOKE DID YOU STICK TO THE TIMES? IF NOT WHY? HOW COULD YOU CHANGE THIS FOR THE FUTURE?

 SESSION 37

5: HOW WAS YOUR BODY LANGUAGE THROUGHOUT THE SESSION BOTH UPPER AND LOWER?

6: HOW MUCH DID YOU LOOK AT PEOPLE IN THE EYES? HOW DID THAT MAKE YOU FEEL? WHAT COULD YOU DO TO HELP THIS FEELING?

7: DID YOU KEEP THE SESSION MOVING OR DID YOU FIND YOURSELF PROCRASTINATING? WHY WAS THIS AND HOW COULD YOU CHANGE THIS FOR NEXT TIME?

8: WHEN THERE WERE SILENCES HOW COMFORTABLE WERE YOU? HOW DID YOU DEAL WITH THIS AND WHAT WOULD YOU LIKE TO BE DIFFERENT FOR NEXT TIME?

9: WRITE ONE POSITIVE AND ONE AREA FOR IMPROVEMENT YOU WILL FOCUS ON IN THE NEXT SESSION. REMEMBER SMALL CHANGES CREATE THE CHANGE.

-
-

GROW YOUR CONFIDENCE WITH PUBLIC SPEAKING JOURNAL

DATE:-   /   /

1: HOW PREPARED WERE YOU BEFORE THE SESSION, PREPARED OR TOO LITTLE? WHAT COULD YOU DO DIFFERENTLY HERE?

2: HOW EARLY DID YOU ENTER THE ROOM? IF YOU SIT IN THE ROOM FOR TEN MINUTES BEFORE HOW COULD YOU USE THIS TIME?

3: HOW GOOD WERE YOUR COMMUNICATION SKILLS TODAY? WHAT WOULD YOU LIKE TO BE DIFFERENT AND HOW CAN YOU START THE CHANGE?

4: WHEN YOU SPOKE DID YOU STICK TO THE TIMES? IF NOT WHY? HOW COULD YOU CHANGE THIS FOR THE FUTURE?

5: HOW WAS YOUR BODY LANGUAGE THROUGHOUT THE SESSION BOTH UPPER AND LOWER?

6: HOW MUCH DID YOU LOOK AT PEOPLE IN THE EYES? HOW DID THAT MAKE YOU FEEL? WHAT COULD YOU DO TO HELP THIS FEELING?

7: DID YOU KEEP THE SESSION MOVING OR DID YOU FIND YOURSELF PROCRASTINATING? WHY WAS THIS AND HOW COULD YOU CHANGE THIS FOR NEXT TIME?

8: WHEN THERE WERE SILENCES HOW COMFORTABLE WERE YOU? HOW DID YOU DEAL WITH THIS AND WHAT WOULD YOU LIKE TO BE DIFFERENT FOR NEXT TIME?

9: WRITE ONE POSITIVE AND ONE AREA FOR IMPROVEMENT YOU WILL FOCUS ON IN THE NEXT SESSION. REMEMBER SMALL CHANGES CREATE THE CHANGE.

-
-

GROW YOUR CONFIDENCE WITH PUBLIC SPEAKING JOURNAL

DATE:-   /   /

1: HOW PREPARED WERE YOU BEFORE THE SESSION, PREPARED OR TOO LITTLE? WHAT COULD YOU DO DIFFERENTLY HERE?

2: HOW EARLY DID YOU ENTER THE ROOM? IF YOU SIT IN THE ROOM FOR TEN MINUTES BEFORE HOW COULD YOU USE THIS TIME?

3: HOW GOOD WERE YOUR COMMUNICATION SKILLS TODAY? WHAT WOULD YOU LIKE TO BE DIFFERENT AND HOW CAN YOU START THE CHANGE?

4: WHEN YOU SPOKE DID YOU STICK TO THE TIMES? IF NOT WHY? HOW COULD YOU CHANGE THIS FOR THE FUTURE?

5: HOW WAS YOUR BODY LANGUAGE THROUGHOUT THE SESSION BOTH UPPER AND LOWER?

6: HOW MUCH DID YOU LOOK AT PEOPLE IN THE EYES? HOW DID THAT MAKE YOU FEEL? WHAT COULD YOU DO TO HELP THIS FEELING?

7: DID YOU KEEP THE SESSION MOVING OR DID YOU FIND YOURSELF PROCRASTINATING? WHY WAS THIS AND HOW COULD YOU CHANGE THIS FOR NEXT TIME?

8: WHEN THERE WERE SILENCES HOW COMFORTABLE WERE YOU? HOW DID YOU DEAL WITH THIS AND WHAT WOULD YOU LIKE TO BE DIFFERENT FOR NEXT TIME?

9: WRITE ONE POSITIVE AND ONE AREA FOR IMPROVEMENT YOU WILL FOCUS ON IN THE NEXT SESSION. REMEMBER SMALL CHANGES CREATE THE CHANGE.

-
-

GROW YOUR CONFIDENCE WITH PUBLIC SPEAKING JOURNAL

DATE:-   /   /

1: HOW PREPARED WERE YOU BEFORE THE SESSION, PREPARED OR TOO LITTLE? WHAT COULD YOU DO DIFFERENTLY HERE?

2: HOW EARLY DID YOU ENTER THE ROOM? IF YOU SIT IN THE ROOM FOR TEN MINUTES BEFORE HOW COULD YOU USE THIS TIME?

3: HOW GOOD WERE YOUR COMMUNICATION SKILLS TODAY? WHAT WOULD YOU LIKE TO BE DIFFERENT AND HOW CAN YOU START THE CHANGE?

4: WHEN YOU SPOKE DID YOU STICK TO THE TIMES? IF NOT WHY? HOW COULD YOU CHANGE THIS FOR THE FUTURE?

5: HOW WAS YOUR BODY LANGUAGE THROUGHOUT THE SESSION BOTH UPPER AND LOWER?

6: HOW MUCH DID YOU LOOK AT PEOPLE IN THE EYES? HOW DID THAT MAKE YOU FEEL? WHAT COULD YOU DO TO HELP THIS FEELING?

7: DID YOU KEEP THE SESSION MOVING OR DID YOU FIND YOURSELF PROCRASTINATING? WHY WAS THIS AND HOW COULD YOU CHANGE THIS FOR NEXT TIME?

8: WHEN THERE WERE SILENCES HOW COMFORTABLE WERE YOU? HOW DID YOU DEAL WITH THIS AND WHAT WOULD YOU LIKE TO BE DIFFERENT FOR NEXT TIME?

9: WRITE ONE POSITIVE AND ONE AREA FOR IMPROVEMENT YOU WILL FOCUS ON IN THE NEXT SESSION. REMEMBER SMALL CHANGES CREATE THE CHANGE.

-
-

GROW YOUR CONFIDENCE WITH PUBLIC SPEAKING JOURNAL

DATE:-   /   /

1: HOW HAVE I GROWN OVER THE LAST 5 SESSIONS?

2: WHAT AM I GOING TO FOCUS ON IN THE NEXT 5 SESSIONS?

3: WHAT FIVE THINGS AM I POSITIVELY TAKING FROM THE LAST FIVE SESSIONS AND MOVING THEM FORWARD?

-
-
-
-
-

4: WHAT KEY AREAS WOULD I LIKE TO CONCENTRATE ON TO IMPROVE FURTHER?

Capture An Audience - If you capture an audience in the first minute you will have them hooked. A really good fact always gets people thinking. Always make it interesting and relevant. If you do this at the start, the audience will be captured.

GROW YOUR CONFIDENCE WITH PUBLIC SPEAKING JOURNAL

DATE:-   /   /

1: HOW PREPARED WERE YOU BEFORE THE SESSION, PREPARED OR TOO LITTLE? WHAT COULD YOU DO DIFFERENTLY HERE?

2: HOW EARLY DID YOU ENTER THE ROOM? IF YOU SIT IN THE ROOM FOR TEN MINUTES BEFORE HOW COULD YOU USE THIS TIME?

3: HOW GOOD WERE YOUR COMMUNICATION SKILLS TODAY? WHAT WOULD YOU LIKE TO BE DIFFERENT AND HOW CAN YOU START THE CHANGE?

4: WHEN YOU SPOKE DID YOU STICK TO THE TIMES? IF NOT WHY? HOW COULD YOU CHANGE THIS FOR THE FUTURE?

5: HOW WAS YOUR BODY LANGUAGE THROUGHOUT THE SESSION BOTH UPPER AND LOWER?

6: HOW MUCH DID YOU LOOK AT PEOPLE IN THE EYES? HOW DID THAT MAKE YOU FEEL? WHAT COULD YOU DO TO HELP THIS FEELING?

7: DID YOU KEEP THE SESSION MOVING OR DID YOU FIND YOURSELF PROCRASTINATING? WHY WAS THIS AND HOW COULD YOU CHANGE THIS FOR NEXT TIME?

8: WHEN THERE WERE SILENCES HOW COMFORTABLE WERE YOU? HOW DID YOU DEAL WITH THIS AND WHAT WOULD YOU LIKE TO BE DIFFERENT FOR NEXT TIME?

9: WRITE ONE POSITIVE AND ONE AREA FOR IMPROVEMENT YOU WILL FOCUS ON IN THE NEXT SESSION. REMEMBER SMALL CHANGES CREATE THE CHANGE.

-
-

GROW YOUR CONFIDENCE WITH PUBLIC SPEAKING JOURNAL

DATE:-   /   /

1: HOW PREPARED WERE YOU BEFORE THE SESSION, PREPARED OR TOO LITTLE? WHAT COULD YOU DO DIFFERENTLY HERE?

2: HOW EARLY DID YOU ENTER THE ROOM? IF YOU SIT IN THE ROOM FOR TEN MINUTES BEFORE HOW COULD YOU USE THIS TIME?

3: HOW GOOD WERE YOUR COMMUNICATION SKILLS TODAY? WHAT WOULD YOU LIKE TO BE DIFFERENT AND HOW CAN YOU START THE CHANGE?

4: WHEN YOU SPOKE DID YOU STICK TO THE TIMES? IF NOT WHY? HOW COULD YOU CHANGE THIS FOR THE FUTURE?

5: HOW WAS YOUR BODY LANGUAGE THROUGHOUT THE SESSION BOTH UPPER AND LOWER?

6: HOW MUCH DID YOU LOOK AT PEOPLE IN THE EYES? HOW DID THAT MAKE YOU FEEL? WHAT COULD YOU DO TO HELP THIS FEELING?

7: DID YOU KEEP THE SESSION MOVING OR DID YOU FIND YOURSELF PROCRASTINATING? WHY WAS THIS AND HOW COULD YOU CHANGE THIS FOR NEXT TIME?

8: WHEN THERE WERE SILENCES HOW COMFORTABLE WERE YOU? HOW DID YOU DEAL WITH THIS AND WHAT WOULD YOU LIKE TO BE DIFFERENT FOR NEXT TIME?

9: WRITE ONE POSITIVE AND ONE AREA FOR IMPROVEMENT YOU WILL FOCUS ON IN THE NEXT SESSION. REMEMBER SMALL CHANGES CREATE THE CHANGE.

-
-

GROW YOUR CONFIDENCE WITH PUBLIC SPEAKING JOURNAL

DATE:- / /

1: HOW PREPARED WERE YOU BEFORE THE SESSION, PREPARED OR TOO LITTLE? WHAT COULD YOU DO DIFFERENTLY HERE?

2: HOW EARLY DID YOU ENTER THE ROOM? IF YOU SIT IN THE ROOM FOR TEN MINUTES BEFORE HOW COULD YOU USE THIS TIME?

3: HOW GOOD WERE YOUR COMMUNICATION SKILLS TODAY? WHAT WOULD YOU LIKE TO BE DIFFERENT AND HOW CAN YOU START THE CHANGE?

4: WHEN YOU SPOKE DID YOU STICK TO THE TIMES? IF NOT WHY? HOW COULD YOU CHANGE THIS FOR THE FUTURE?

5: HOW WAS YOUR BODY LANGUAGE THROUGHOUT THE SESSION BOTH UPPER AND LOWER?

6: HOW MUCH DID YOU LOOK AT PEOPLE IN THE EYES? HOW DID THAT MAKE YOU FEEL? WHAT COULD YOU DO TO HELP THIS FEELING?

7: DID YOU KEEP THE SESSION MOVING OR DID YOU FIND YOURSELF PROCRASTINATING? WHY WAS THIS AND HOW COULD YOU CHANGE THIS FOR NEXT TIME?

8: WHEN THERE WERE SILENCES HOW COMFORTABLE WERE YOU? HOW DID YOU DEAL WITH THIS AND WHAT WOULD YOU LIKE TO BE DIFFERENT FOR NEXT TIME?

9: WRITE ONE POSITIVE AND ONE AREA FOR IMPROVEMENT YOU WILL FOCUS ON IN THE NEXT SESSION. REMEMBER SMALL CHANGES CREATE THE CHANGE.

-
-

GROW YOUR CONFIDENCE WITH PUBLIC SPEAKING JOURNAL

DATE:-   /   /

1: HOW PREPARED WERE YOU BEFORE THE SESSION, PREPARED OR TOO LITTLE? WHAT COULD YOU DO DIFFERENTLY HERE?

2: HOW EARLY DID YOU ENTER THE ROOM? IF YOU SIT IN THE ROOM FOR TEN MINUTES BEFORE HOW COULD YOU USE THIS TIME?

3: HOW GOOD WERE YOUR COMMUNICATION SKILLS TODAY? WHAT WOULD YOU LIKE TO BE DIFFERENT AND HOW CAN YOU START THE CHANGE?

4: WHEN YOU SPOKE DID YOU STICK TO THE TIMES? IF NOT WHY? HOW COULD YOU CHANGE THIS FOR THE FUTURE?

5: HOW WAS YOUR BODY LANGUAGE THROUGHOUT THE SESSION BOTH UPPER AND LOWER?

6: HOW MUCH DID YOU LOOK AT PEOPLE IN THE EYES? HOW DID THAT MAKE YOU FEEL? WHAT COULD YOU DO TO HELP THIS FEELING?

7: DID YOU KEEP THE SESSION MOVING OR DID YOU FIND YOURSELF PROCRASTINATING? WHY WAS THIS AND HOW COULD YOU CHANGE THIS FOR NEXT TIME?

8: WHEN THERE WERE SILENCES HOW COMFORTABLE WERE YOU? HOW DID YOU DEAL WITH THIS AND WHAT WOULD YOU LIKE TO BE DIFFERENT FOR NEXT TIME?

9: WRITE ONE POSITIVE AND ONE AREA FOR IMPROVEMENT YOU WILL FOCUS ON IN THE NEXT SESSION. REMEMBER SMALL CHANGES CREATE THE CHANGE.

GROW YOUR CONFIDENCE WITH PUBLIC SPEAKING JOURNAL

DATE:-   /   /

1: HOW PREPARED WERE YOU BEFORE THE SESSION, PREPARED OR TOO LITTLE? WHAT COULD YOU DO DIFFERENTLY HERE?

2: HOW EARLY DID YOU ENTER THE ROOM? IF YOU SIT IN THE ROOM FOR TEN MINUTES BEFORE HOW COULD YOU USE THIS TIME?

3: HOW GOOD WERE YOUR COMMUNICATION SKILLS TODAY? WHAT WOULD YOU LIKE TO BE DIFFERENT AND HOW CAN YOU START THE CHANGE?

4: WHEN YOU SPOKE DID YOU STICK TO THE TIMES? IF NOT WHY? HOW COULD YOU CHANGE THIS FOR THE FUTURE?

5: HOW WAS YOUR BODY LANGUAGE THROUGHOUT THE SESSION BOTH UPPER AND LOWER?

6: HOW MUCH DID YOU LOOK AT PEOPLE IN THE EYES? HOW DID THAT MAKE YOU FEEL? WHAT COULD YOU DO TO HELP THIS FEELING?

7: DID YOU KEEP THE SESSION MOVING OR DID YOU FIND YOURSELF PROCRASTINATING? WHY WAS THIS AND HOW COULD YOU CHANGE THIS FOR NEXT TIME?

8: WHEN THERE WERE SILENCES HOW COMFORTABLE WERE YOU? HOW DID YOU DEAL WITH THIS AND WHAT WOULD YOU LIKE TO BE DIFFERENT FOR NEXT TIME?

9: WRITE ONE POSITIVE AND ONE AREA FOR IMPROVEMENT YOU WILL FOCUS ON IN THE NEXT SESSION. REMEMBER SMALL CHANGES CREATE THE CHANGE.

1: HOW HAVE I GROWN OVER THE LAST 5 SESSIONS?

2: WHAT AM I GOING TO FOCUS ON IN THE NEXT 5 SESSIONS?

3: WHAT FIVE THINGS AM I POSITIVELY TAKING FROM THE LAST FIVE SESSIONS AND MOVING THEM FORWARD?

-
-
-
-
-

4: WHAT KEY AREAS WOULD I LIKE TO CONCENTRATE ON TO IMPROVE FURTHER?

Use The 'B' Button -
When using PowerPoint use the
'B' button on the keyboard. This
blanks the PowerPoint slide and
you can even walk in front of a
projector with no light (or slide)
on you! It sends a message to
the group to focus on the trainer

DATE:-   /   /

1: HOW PREPARED WERE YOU BEFORE THE SESSION, PREPARED OR TOO LITTLE? WHAT COULD YOU DO DIFFERENTLY HERE?

2: HOW EARLY DID YOU ENTER THE ROOM? IF YOU SIT IN THE ROOM FOR TEN MINUTES BEFORE HOW COULD YOU USE THIS TIME?

3: HOW GOOD WERE YOUR COMMUNICATION SKILLS TODAY? WHAT WOULD YOU LIKE TO BE DIFFERENT AND HOW CAN YOU START THE CHANGE?

4: WHEN YOU SPOKE DID YOU STICK TO THE TIMES? IF NOT WHY? HOW COULD YOU CHANGE THIS FOR THE FUTURE?

5: HOW WAS YOUR BODY LANGUAGE THROUGHOUT THE SESSION BOTH UPPER AND LOWER?

6: HOW MUCH DID YOU LOOK AT PEOPLE IN THE EYES? HOW DID THAT MAKE YOU FEEL? WHAT COULD YOU DO TO HELP THIS FEELING?

7: DID YOU KEEP THE SESSION MOVING OR DID YOU FIND YOURSELF PROCRASTINATING? WHY WAS THIS AND HOW COULD YOU CHANGE THIS FOR NEXT TIME?

8: WHEN THERE WERE SILENCES HOW COMFORTABLE WERE YOU? HOW DID YOU DEAL WITH THIS AND WHAT WOULD YOU LIKE TO BE DIFFERENT FOR NEXT TIME?

9: WRITE ONE POSITIVE AND ONE AREA FOR IMPROVEMENT YOU WILL FOCUS ON IN THE NEXT SESSION. REMEMBER SMALL CHANGES CREATE THE CHANGE.

-
-

GROW YOUR CONFIDENCE WITH PUBLIC SPEAKING JOURNAL

DATE:-   /   /

1: HOW PREPARED WERE YOU BEFORE THE SESSION, PREPARED OR TOO LITTLE? WHAT COULD YOU DO DIFFERENTLY HERE?

2: HOW EARLY DID YOU ENTER THE ROOM? IF YOU SIT IN THE ROOM FOR TEN MINUTES BEFORE HOW COULD YOU USE THIS TIME?

3: HOW GOOD WERE YOUR COMMUNICATION SKILLS TODAY? WHAT WOULD YOU LIKE TO BE DIFFERENT AND HOW CAN YOU START THE CHANGE?

4: WHEN YOU SPOKE DID YOU STICK TO THE TIMES? IF NOT WHY? HOW COULD YOU CHANGE THIS FOR THE FUTURE?

5: HOW WAS YOUR BODY LANGUAGE THROUGHOUT THE SESSION BOTH UPPER AND LOWER?

6: HOW MUCH DID YOU LOOK AT PEOPLE IN THE EYES? HOW DID THAT MAKE YOU FEEL? WHAT COULD YOU DO TO HELP THIS FEELING?

7: DID YOU KEEP THE SESSION MOVING OR DID YOU FIND YOURSELF PROCRASTINATING? WHY WAS THIS AND HOW COULD YOU CHANGE THIS FOR NEXT TIME?

8: WHEN THERE WERE SILENCES HOW COMFORTABLE WERE YOU? HOW DID YOU DEAL WITH THIS AND WHAT WOULD YOU LIKE TO BE DIFFERENT FOR NEXT TIME?

9: WRITE ONE POSITIVE AND ONE AREA FOR IMPROVEMENT YOU WILL FOCUS ON IN THE NEXT SESSION. REMEMBER SMALL CHANGES CREATE THE CHANGE.

GROW YOUR CONFIDENCE WITH PUBLIC SPEAKING JOURNAL

DATE:-   /   /

1: HOW PREPARED WERE YOU BEFORE THE SESSION, PREPARED OR TOO LITTLE? WHAT COULD YOU DO DIFFERENTLY HERE?

2: HOW EARLY DID YOU ENTER THE ROOM? IF YOU SIT IN THE ROOM FOR TEN MINUTES BEFORE HOW COULD YOU USE THIS TIME?

3: HOW GOOD WERE YOUR COMMUNICATION SKILLS TODAY? WHAT WOULD YOU LIKE TO BE DIFFERENT AND HOW CAN YOU START THE CHANGE?

4: WHEN YOU SPOKE DID YOU STICK TO THE TIMES? IF NOT WHY? HOW COULD YOU CHANGE THIS FOR THE FUTURE?

5: HOW WAS YOUR BODY LANGUAGE THROUGHOUT THE SESSION BOTH UPPER AND LOWER?

6: HOW MUCH DID YOU LOOK AT PEOPLE IN THE EYES? HOW DID THAT MAKE YOU FEEL? WHAT COULD YOU DO TO HELP THIS FEELING?

7: DID YOU KEEP THE SESSION MOVING OR DID YOU FIND YOURSELF PROCRASTINATING? WHY WAS THIS AND HOW COULD YOU CHANGE THIS FOR NEXT TIME?

8: WHEN THERE WERE SILENCES HOW COMFORTABLE WERE YOU? HOW DID YOU DEAL WITH THIS AND WHAT WOULD YOU LIKE TO BE DIFFERENT FOR NEXT TIME?

9: WRITE ONE POSITIVE AND ONE AREA FOR IMPROVEMENT YOU WILL FOCUS ON IN THE NEXT SESSION. REMEMBER SMALL CHANGES CREATE THE CHANGE.

-
-

GROW YOUR CONFIDENCE WITH PUBLIC SPEAKING JOURNAL

DATE:-   /   /

1: HOW PREPARED WERE YOU BEFORE THE SESSION, PREPARED OR TOO LITTLE? WHAT COULD YOU DO DIFFERENTLY HERE?

2: HOW EARLY DID YOU ENTER THE ROOM? IF YOU SIT IN THE ROOM FOR TEN MINUTES BEFORE HOW COULD YOU USE THIS TIME?

3: HOW GOOD WERE YOUR COMMUNICATION SKILLS TODAY? WHAT WOULD YOU LIKE TO BE DIFFERENT AND HOW CAN YOU START THE CHANGE?

4: WHEN YOU SPOKE DID YOU STICK TO THE TIMES? IF NOT WHY? HOW COULD YOU CHANGE THIS FOR THE FUTURE?

5: HOW WAS YOUR BODY LANGUAGE THROUGHOUT THE SESSION BOTH UPPER AND LOWER?

6: HOW MUCH DID YOU LOOK AT PEOPLE IN THE EYES? HOW DID THAT MAKE YOU FEEL? WHAT COULD YOU DO TO HELP THIS FEELING?

7: DID YOU KEEP THE SESSION MOVING OR DID YOU FIND YOURSELF PROCRASTINATING? WHY WAS THIS AND HOW COULD YOU CHANGE THIS FOR NEXT TIME?

8: WHEN THERE WERE SILENCES HOW COMFORTABLE WERE YOU? HOW DID YOU DEAL WITH THIS AND WHAT WOULD YOU LIKE TO BE DIFFERENT FOR NEXT TIME?

9: WRITE ONE POSITIVE AND ONE AREA FOR IMPROVEMENT YOU WILL FOCUS ON IN THE NEXT SESSION. REMEMBER SMALL CHANGES CREATE THE CHANGE.

GROW YOUR CONFIDENCE WITH PUBLIC SPEAKING JOURNAL

DATE:-   /   /

1: HOW PREPARED WERE YOU BEFORE THE SESSION, PREPARED OR TOO LITTLE? WHAT COULD YOU DO DIFFERENTLY HERE?

2: HOW EARLY DID YOU ENTER THE ROOM? IF YOU SIT IN THE ROOM FOR TEN MINUTES BEFORE HOW COULD YOU USE THIS TIME?

3: HOW GOOD WERE YOUR COMMUNICATION SKILLS TODAY? WHAT WOULD YOU LIKE TO BE DIFFERENT AND HOW CAN YOU START THE CHANGE?

4: WHEN YOU SPOKE DID YOU STICK TO THE TIMES? IF NOT WHY? HOW COULD YOU CHANGE THIS FOR THE FUTURE?

5: HOW WAS YOUR BODY LANGUAGE THROUGHOUT THE SESSION BOTH UPPER AND LOWER?

6: HOW MUCH DID YOU LOOK AT PEOPLE IN THE EYES? HOW DID THAT MAKE YOU FEEL? WHAT COULD YOU DO TO HELP THIS FEELING?

7: DID YOU KEEP THE SESSION MOVING OR DID YOU FIND YOURSELF PROCRASTINATING? WHY WAS THIS AND HOW COULD YOU CHANGE THIS FOR NEXT TIME?

8: WHEN THERE WERE SILENCES HOW COMFORTABLE WERE YOU? HOW DID YOU DEAL WITH THIS AND WHAT WOULD YOU LIKE TO BE DIFFERENT FOR NEXT TIME?

9: WRITE ONE POSITIVE AND ONE AREA FOR IMPROVEMENT YOU WILL FOCUS ON IN THE NEXT SESSION. REMEMBER SMALL CHANGES CREATE THE CHANGE.

-
-

DATE:-
/ /

1: HOW HAVE I GROWN OVER THE LAST 5 SESSIONS?

2: WHAT AM I GOING TO FOCUS ON IN THE NEXT 5 SESSIONS?

3: WHAT FIVE THINGS AM I POSITIVELY TAKING FROM THE LAST FIVE SESSIONS AND MOVING THEM FORWARD?

-
-
-
-
-

4: WHAT KEY AREAS WOULD I LIKE TO CONCENTRATE ON TO IMPROVE FURTHER?

Session 50

Congratulations

Congratulations on achieving 50 sessions of public speaking reflection. You have completed and reflected on your practice. You have our permission to give yourself an award for achieving this fantastic milestone. Now think about how you can take this forward and grow further, amazing stuff.

WRITE FIVE THINGS THAT YOU HAVE BECOME MUCH MORE AWARE OF. THE JOURNAL HAS GIVEN YOU LITTLE SPACES TO WRITE KEY THINGS DOWN, OBVIOUSLY THE GREATER THE REFLECTION THE MORE YOU IMPROVE. THE PROBLEM IS NOT EVERYONE IS AWARE WRITING DOWN WORKS, THIS JOURNAL KEEPS IT EASY FOR YOU.

GOOD LUCK WITH MOVING FORWARD, BE PROUD OF YOURSELF.

1...

2...

3...

4...

5...

If you have enjoyed this journal please leave us a review on Amazon.

NOTES

NOTES

JCRM JOURNALS
MEET THE AUTHORS

www.jcrmjournals.com

RALPH MOODY

Ralph believes that lifelong learning is precisely that, and should not be limited by age or perceived ability. He has a belief that all of us have the potential to do anything if we put our minds to it. Armed with the right skills, knowledge and attitude, we can all perform to the highest standards. Moreover, his philosophy is that limiting belief is what holds the majority of people back and that, with appropriate coaching, mentoring and training, we can all achieve anything. With over 30 years of training experience, he specialises in trainer, management and leadership development.

> *"Life is a gift and we all have a responsibility to make the most of it, so that when we look back, we know it wasn't wasted"*
>
> RALPH MOODY

CLAIRE MOODY

Claire is an extremely experienced trainer and coach at Target Training, and you can always guarantee she will deliver outstanding results: she is incredibly passionate about both her training and coaching. She has over 35 years' experience in training, coaching and quality assurance roles, with experience as a teacher and in Train the Trainer, working with international clients. Moreover, she has expertise in the management of trainer inductions, standardisation and quality assurance for corporate clients. She holds an MSc in executive coaching and is accredited by Ashridge, a world leader in executive coach training and development. Additionally, she specialises in psychometric assessment, including MBTI.

> *"It's not about being the best, it's about being the best you can be"*
>
> CLAIRE MOODY

HAVE QUESTIONS?

Target Training Associates
107 Cheapside, London, EC2V 6DN
0800 302 9344
info@targettrg.co.uk
www.targettrg.co.uk
www.jcrmjournals.com

SOME OTHER TITLES IN THE JOURNAL SERIES

Coaching Journal
Training Journal
Being Positive Journal
Improve Self-Esteem Journal
Do I or don't I deal with conflict Journal
Action Planning Journal
Management Journal
Rainbow Foods Journal

Contact us for a quote for a bespoke journal for your particular organisation